THE
GUIDEBOOK
FOR THE
OVERCOMER

A DEVOTIONAL EXPOSITION OF PSALM 119

"He who overcomes will not be hurt by the second death."
REVELATION 2:11

"I came that they may have life, and have it abundantly."
JOHN 10:10B

KENNETH P. WALDOCK

Wasteland Press
www.wastelandpress.net
Shelbyville, KY USA

The Guidebook for the Overcomer:
A Devotional Exposition of Psalm 119
by Kenneth P. Waldock

First Printing – February 2024
ISBN: 978-1-68111-553-5

Printed in the U.S.A.

0   1   2   3

Dedicated to my wife, Mary.

"Her children rise up and bless her;
Her husband also, and he praises her,
saying,
'Many daughters have done nobly
but you excel them all.'"

Proverbs 31:28, 29 (NASB)

Table of Contents

Introduction

The summer between my junior and senior year in college, my pastor was preaching through Psalm 119 during the Wednesday evening prayer meeting before we all broke away for prayer. My pastor was an excellent expositor of the scriptures, and I was duly impressed by his ability to preach through this psalm.

I had always been intrigued by Psalm 119 as nearly every verse has a reference to the Word of God and because each stanza has an acrostic pattern. However, I thought it would be rather difficult to preach one stanza at a time as I thought the eight verses of each stanza pretty much stood alone. So, I had to determine whether there is a prevailing thought for each stanza of eight verses.

Years later, as I began my ministry at a church plant in India, I decided to see if I could preach through Psalm 119 during Wednesday evening prayer meetings. This book is the result of that initial effort and the refinement that came over the years as I taught or preached through this psalm in seminary chapel, home Bible studies, men's Bible studies, and Sunday school. The richness of Psalm 119 has made a deep impression on me and provided the motivation for me to be a student of God's Word for more than just sermon preparation.

There is some uncertainty as to who the human author is, but Charles H. Spurgeon was convinced it was King David. I tend to agree with him, though one cannot be dogmatic. There is a kinship with Psalm 19, written by David, that would suggest Psalm 119 was also written by him. Also, when reading the psalms of David, one cannot help but notice his love for God's Word, which led to him being a "man after God's own heart." A careful study of and meditation on Psalm 119 will draw one closer to the heart of God.

The Psalm is divided into twenty-two stanzas according to the Hebrew alphabet, in Hebrew alphabetic order. Each stanza has eight verses, and each verse starts with the letter of the Hebrew alphabet corresponding to the stanza in which it is found.

This psalm is a beautiful example of Hebrew poetry, which is much different than traditional English poetry of rhyme and meter.

1. Hebrew poetry normally consists of two lines, or a couplet, that complement each other. We call this parallelisms.

2. There are four basic parallel structures:

    a. Synonymous parallelism — the second line of poetry expresses the same thought as the first line with different words. Psalm 119:105

    b. Synthetic parallelism — the second line of poetry expands on the thought in the first line. Psalm 119:11

    c. Antithetic parallelism — the second line of poetry expresses an opposite thought compared to the first line. Psalm 119:3

    d. Chiastic parallelism — this is the same as synonymous parallelism except the second line makes the predicate the subject, and the subject becomes the predicate. Psalm 119:111

The general theme of the psalm is the dynamics of the Word of God in a person's life. Scholars differ as to how many synonyms are used for the scriptures, but I have focused on eight. Nearly every verse has at least one synonym for the scriptures, and the few that do not will be noted in the exposition. The following chart shows the eight terms with their meanings from the Hebrew and how various translations have rendered them.

Psalm 119 Definitions

HEBREW	KJV	NASB	ESV	DEFINITION
dabar	word	word	word	word, thing, matter
mitzvah	commandment	commandment	commandment	
amar	word	word	promise	word, promise or saying, order (keep one's word)
chukah	statute	statute	statute	something decreed or fixed or established an act of a corporation or of its founder intended as a permanent rule
pekudim	precepts/statutes	precepts	precepts	directions, orders (military) — precision and authority
torah	law	law	law	The Law, law, directions, instructions (revealed will)
mishphat	judgments	ordinances/judgments	rules	judgment — decision by arbitration, legal/judicial decision
eduth	testimonies	testimonies	testimonies	warning signs, reminders, urgings — truth attested by God

The Hebrew definitions are derived from "A Concise Hebrew and Aramaic Lexicon of the Old Testament" by William Holladay published by Eerdmans in 1971.

I have chosen the New American Standard Bible as the text for the exposition, and when the NASB uses the word "ordinances," I have replaced it with [judgments] for consistency and to retain the meaning within the context of the passage.

The psalm develops the theme of the necessity of adhering to the Word of God to experience the abundant life Jesus came to offer (John 10:10). However, each stanza can stand alone, and I have developed each one as a separate unit. Therefore, there is a fair amount of redundancy found throughout the exposition.

I have called this a devotional exposition as I have tried to use illustrations and applications not normally found in other expositions or commentaries. Each stanza can be used as a devotional or lesson separately. It is my desire that the reader will have a better understanding of the psalm and that it will touch his heart with the awesome relevance of the Bible for our walk with the Lord Jesus Christ even in the age in which we live.

Psalm 119:1–8 — Aleph

God's Personal Attention

א

Aleph.

1   How blessed are those whose way is blameless,
    Who walk in the law of the LORD.
2   How blessed are those who observe His testimonies,
    Who seek Him with all *their* heart.
3   They also do no unrighteousness;
    They walk in His ways.

4   You have ordained Your precepts,
    That we should keep *them* diligently.

5   Oh that my ways may be established
    To keep Your statutes!
6   Then I shall not be ashamed
    When I look upon all Your commandments.
7   I shall give thanks to You with uprightness of heart,
    When I learn Your righteous judgments.
8   I shall keep Your statutes;
    Do not forsake me utterly![1]

We often speak of God's love for us, and the scriptures affirm God's love many times over. One of the characteristics of love is that it

---

[1] *New American Standard Bible: 1995 update*. 1995 (Psalm 119:1–8). LaHabra, CA: The Lockman Foundation.

cannot be impersonal or aloof. This is also true of God. He loves us, and that love is demonstrated through His personal attention to each of us. One problem, though, is we want God to demonstrate His love to us according to our wishes and demands. God, on the other hand, demonstrates His love to us according to what is in our best interests. The spiritually wise person will seek to discover how God demonstrates His love and then seek to understand how that demonstration of His love is in his best interests. The search begins with Scripture because God speaks through His Word. Psalm 119 extols the virtues of God's Word and at the same time demonstrates that, by giving us His Word, God truly has our best interests in mind.

This first portion of Psalm 119 explains how God demonstrates His love for us through His personal attention.

God delights in our righteousness (verses 1–3)
God shows that He delights in our righteousness by blessing us. The psalmist cries out, *"How blessed are those whose way is blameless."* When we live righteously it does not escape God's attention and He blesses us. The blessed person is one who is truly happy. The happiness is not based on circumstances but on a sense of being in a right relationship with God. Some have even suggested the blessed person is one who is to be envied by others. We envy those who exhibit peace and contentment in their daily lives. While they still have hardships and difficulties, they experience God's blessing and approval no matter what happens in their lives.

The prerequisite for experiencing God's blessing is that our way, or life, has to be blameless. The definition of "blameless" or "undefiled" is found in verse one, *"Who walk in the law of the Lord."*

Let's take a closer look at some key words. The word "way" is sometimes translated as "path," and a path is defined as a stretch of land that has become a path by being frequented. I take great comfort in knowing the path I take in life is one that many others have been on, as well. I doubt any of us are true trailblazers especially in our walk as believers. A path is also clearly discernible. We do not have to stumble around searching for it.

Verse 1 tells us this path is clearly laid out for us in the law of the Lord, that is, the Word of God. Therefore, if we walk life's pathway according to the Word of God, we will be blameless or undefiled, and if we are blameless God shows His delight in us by blessing us. One can only be blameless if he conducts his life according to the Word of God and one can only be happy by being blameless.

But what does it mean specifically to *"walk in the law of the Lord?"* Verse 2 declares that the ones who are blessed are those who observe God's testimonies. Following the principles of Hebrew poetic parallelism, this is simply another way of saying the same thing. The next few lines expand on what is meant by observing (keeping, complying with) God's testimonies:

1. *"Who seek Him with all their heart."* The words "to seek" mean to be intent on something or someone. When a person observes God's testimonies, he is intently seeking after God. His intensity is indicated by an undivided or a singleness of heart. This means his whole life is focused on the pursuit of God and His ways. Such a person will also be conscious that God sees how sincere the heart is.

2. *"They also do no unrighteousness."* That is, they don't do any unrighteousness. All it takes is one misstep for us to experience a loss of blessedness.

3. *"They walk in His ways."* If we walk in His ways, we will not commit unrighteous acts. Going back to what I said concerning verse 1, note that a) God's way is a path that has been frequented, not just by other believers but by God

7

Himself. This takes on more significance for the New Testament believer because Jesus, God in the flesh, walked this earth and fulfilled all righteousness. He has walked the same path He asks us to walk. He does not ask us to do something He has not already done; and b) God's way is a path that He has clearly marked. We are not walking in uncharted territory.

In other words, God wants to bless us, so He clearly tells us how we can lead a blameless life. He is not so cruel as to demand something that is obscure or unreachable. He loves us and wants to bless us.

Let's look at another way that God demonstrates His love for us through personal attention.

God demands our obedience (verse 4)
God is not an aloof parent who does not care what we do or what happens to us. God has ordained or laid down His precepts. The word "precepts" means directions or orders and is usually in the context of military orders. In the army the orders of an officer are carried out without question. Only a higher-ranking officer can countermand an order of a lower-ranking officer. God is the highest-ranking officer. No one can change His orders. He expects us to carry them out, and He expects us to carry them out diligently, not half-heartedly. Alfred Barnes says in his commentary, "Each one of His laws is to be observed, and to be observed always, and to be observed in all circumstances." (Barnes, 1950)

We may take heart that God is a compassionate, commanding officer who does not bark out commands that are of no purpose or of malicious intent. They are for our good and for our blessedness. He loves us so much that He gives His orders and demands our obedience because He knows what is best for us.

The remainder of this "Aleph" portion gives us one last demonstration of God's personal attention characteristic of His love for us.

God desires our perseverance (verses 5–8)

God wants us to succeed. God has never desired to see us fail, and it doesn't make sense for God to demand anything of us that He knows we will never be able to accomplish. Still, success takes effort, and the pathway is not always easy. God provides the direction and strength, but it is up to us to persevere knowing that success is possible with God's help.

1. The necessity of a personal desire (verses 5–6)
   Look at the psalmist's cry, *"Oh that my ways may be established to keep Your statutes."* He indicates a prevailing desire to keep God's statutes. He knows there may be failures, but the desire prevails. Again, we see the word "way." Throughout life's journey it is the psalmist's firm desire to have his life established on the principles of God's Word.

   When this is true, he will not be ashamed when he has a consideration for all of God's commandments. His desire is to be faithful to all of them, not to pick and choose those that are convenient for him. Then there would be no occasion to be ashamed. God clearly reveals His commands so that they are available to all people. No one needs to spend a lifetime searching for them (Deuteronomy 30:11–16).

   One need never be ashamed for doing right, which is God's will (Cf. Psalm 97:7). That is, we will never have to be ashamed before God. The choice is ours, shame before God or before men (I John 2:28; 4:17). Many would rather avoid shame (or embarrassment) before men only to find they are ashamed at the coming of the Lord Jesus.

God requires us to intend to keep His commands and have a strong desire to do so. We take comfort in knowing that God's faithfulness endures despite our imperfections and that God knows our hearts.

2. The necessity of a personal determination (verses 7–8)
    "I shall give thanks to you." This appears to be a statement of determination rather than of fact. (The Hebrew text suggests this is a hiphil, imperfect, cohortative.)
    We can give true praise or thanksgiving to God only when our hearts are upright or clean. It makes one wonder how much praise in a worship service is acceptable! Not only do we need clean lives, but our praise is most significant when we are continually learning God's righteous judgments. God's judgments are always right and fair, and as we learn, we have more cause to be determined to praise Him. Therefore, if we are determined to give thanks, we will be in the process of learning.

    Learning takes method and time. It takes three basic steps:
    a) Study — we will study God's Word to derive the meaning.
    b) Meditation — we meditate on the meaning to assimilate scripture into our thought processes and world view.
    c) Practice — we apply the truth to our lives.

    I can draw two conclusions to this. Praise without continual learning tends to be extremely shallow, so more learning results in more praise. If our study of scripture does not lead to more praise and thanksgiving, then something has short-circuited our learning process. Do not ever stop learning.

"I shall keep Your statutes." Again, this makes more sense if it is understood as the psalmist's determination to keep God's statutes rather than just a statement of fact.

God's statutes are to be taken here as a synonym for the entire Word of God and not just for those portions that are designated as laws of conduct for Israel.

Even with the determination to keep God's Word there is the cry for God's enablement to do so, *"Don't forsake me utterly!"* God is faithful in that He will never leave us or forsake us. He is always there to give us the understanding, strength, and encouragement to keep His Word. Truly, He answers the prayer of one who sincerely desires to keep His Word.

God does love us. He wants us to succeed in keeping His ways so that we may experience His blessing in our lives. Our part to play is having the strong desire to learn, obey, and trust God for His enablement.

This sets the tone for the whole Psalm. Its similarity to the Psalm 1 is remarkable in that the blessed man is one who lives according to the Word of God. As we progress through this Psalm, we will find that blessedness is not devoid of difficult or dangerous situations but that the man of God is blessed by being under the watchful care of a loving God.

Psalm 119:9–16 — Beth

The Well-balanced Christian Life

ב

Beth.

9   How can a young man keep his way pure?
    By keeping *it* according to Your word.
10 With all my heart I have sought You;
    Do not let me wander from Your commandments.
11 Your word I have treasured in my heart,
    That I may not sin against You.

12 Blessed are You, O LORD;
    Teach me Your statutes.
13 With my lips I have told of
    All the [judgments] of Your mouth.
14 I have rejoiced in the way of Your testimonies,
    As much as in all riches.

15 I will meditate on Your precepts
    And regard Your ways.
16 I shall delight in Your statutes;
    I shall not forget Your word.[2]

Though God leads us by His Word, we would be naive to think the Christian journey is easy. The path before us is strewn with dangers,

---

[2] *New American Standard Bible: 1995 update*. 1995 (Psalm 119:9–16). LaHabra, CA: The Lockman Foundation.

stumbling blocks, enticing diversions, and pitfalls. If I love God, I will have a desire to keep on the path. It will be the desire of my heart to keep from falling. However, I know I am human, and I will make mistakes no matter how good my intentions are. I take great comfort in knowing that God knows not only my weaknesses but also the intent of my heart. In fact, I believe He is more concerned with the attitude of my heart and is compassionate enough not to get upset with my weaknesses and failures.

This section of Psalm 119 describes a godly man who demonstrates his love for God. It is one thing to say we love God, but it is another matter to demonstrate that love in tangible ways. God knows the sincerity of our hearts, but do we? And do others? There are three ways we can demonstrate our love for God.

We demonstrate a concern for righteousness (verses 9–11)

1. Purity (verse 9)

    "How can a young man keep his way pure?" The psalmist seems to be an old man ready to instruct young men (and women) who are starting life's journey as adults who sincerely desire to lead godly lives. Some translations seem to be asking how to be cleansed of past sins. Our text, however, provides the right meaning, which is the desire to know the secret to living a blameless life, especially after verse 1 says God blesses the blameless person. Certainly one desires to have God's blessing on his life. Regardless of how old a person is, if he loves the Lord, he will demonstrate that love by a sincere desire to lead a pure life before God.

    The answer to the question is immediately given, *"By keeping it according to Your word."* Simply put, it means to pay attention to God's Word. Just reading God's Word each day, though a good habit, is really not enough. The person who loves God will read and pay attention to God's Word so that he may conduct his life by it.

2. Prayer (verse 10)

   The psalmist starts with a statement of fact, *"with all my heart I have sought You."* This is not a boast. He knows that God sees his heart and knows whether it is true or not. He is simply stating that he seeks after God with an undivided heart, reaffirming what he said in verse 2. He is not serving God and wealth (Matthew 6:24). He is not pursuing personal ambitions at the expense of God's will for his life. He is simply, to the best of his ability and in the sincerity of his heart, seeking God wholeheartedly.

   However, he is aware of his human tendency to falter even with the best of intentions, and therefore he prays, *"Do not let me wander from Your commandments."* A sincere heart will not be an arrogant or overconfident heart, but it certainly could be an apprehensive heart. No matter how good our intentions, we will recognize that we are prone to wander, so we turn to the Lord to help us keep to the way of His truth.

3. Purpose (verse 11)

   God will certainly aid us in our quest if we show our sincerity by doing what we can to remain true to Him. *"Your word I have treasured in my heart"* demonstrates that the psalmist is going to be engaged in the process. He purposefully stores up God's Word in his innermost being as a treasure, recognizing that a life grounded in God's Word will help preserve him from the pitfalls ahead. What better way to demonstrate the intent of our hearts than to pursue the integration of God's Word into the very fabric of our lives?

A person who loves God will demonstrate that love by being genuinely concerned about living a pure life that is pleasing to the Lord. He relies on the power of the Word and prayer to fortify his resolve to live a righteous life.

We demonstrate a continual rejoicing (verses 12–14)

1. Praise in worship (verse 12)

   Our psalmist bursts out with, *"Blessed are You, O Lord."* There seems to be an abrupt change in subject matter, but when we consider that he is a godly man, who desires to live a pure life, we can assume he has absolute confidence in God's desire to answer his prayer by helping him in his quest. This would be an appropriate outburst of praise in worship that God has heard the cry of his heart.

   True worship will result in a longing for more instruction, *"Teach me your statutes."* He prays that God will continue to teach him, which will equip him for the journey of life before him. The customary order of our worship services now makes sense. As the believers sing and pray in genuine worship, they will naturally be ready for instruction from the Word of God. The lack of hunger for God's Word might be a reflection on our worship, which in turn might indicate an indifference to a blameless walk before God.

2. Praise in proclamation (verse 13)

   Once we have been filled with the experience of genuine worship, the normal response will be to tell others of our great God. When we tell others about God, we share what He has revealed about Himself through His Word. It is important that we faithfully represent Him in our proclamation of Him. We become the oral transmitter of the judgments that came from the mouth of God.

Allow me to point out once again the natural sequence of events here. Praise and worship lead to a desire for more learning, and having learned, we cannot keep it to ourselves. We must proclaim it to others.

3. Praise in perspective (verse 14)
    When the psalmist considers the way of God's testimonies, he rejoices. When we understand what he means by testimonies, we will see why he rejoices. At first the idea has to do with someone's personal testimony of his first-hand experience. Remember, we have found that God Himself, in the person of His Son, along with others, have travelled the path we travel along. God gives us His personal testimony of how things really are. This testimony then acts as urgings to follow the same pathway or warnings of the pitfalls ahead.

    I discovered the truth of this verse during my experiences of driving in Bangalore, India. There was a certain street I used quite frequently that had an abrupt right-hand turn at the end of it. As I was familiar with the street, it did not come as a surprise, but one day I noticed there was actually a sign warning me of an abrupt right turn ahead. The problem was I saw the sign was located only after I had to negotiate the turn! So, it does not do the driver any good at all. God's warning signs are timely. He does not say, "Oops, I was going to warn you about that curve, but I forgot."

    Also, in Bangalore, those responsible for the roads love putting speed bumps in the most obscure places. They do not paint them, so they blend in with the pavement, and there are usually no warning signs that one is ahead. It seems most of them are placed in the shade of trees which makes them even more difficult to anticipate. People driving motorcycles and scooters have lost their lives by hitting them at an inappropriate speed. I have broken the suspension on my Jeep and gotten whiplash from hitting these speed bumps. Most of the time I am aware of where they are, so I can be careful, but the road crews will put them up without any warning, and a familiar road becomes an accident waiting to happen. Occasionally they do paint them or have warning signs next to them, so I understand why anyone would rejoice in warning signs.

Another spiritual lesson I have learned relates to the previous paragraph. We can get so overconfident on the road we are on that we fail to be alert to the new traps our enemy can spring on us. Praise the Lord, His Word always provides timely warning signs for us to follow based on the testimony of one who has been there before us.

The psalmist says he rejoices in the way of God's testimonies, *"As much as in all riches."* Another way of rendering that last phrase would be, *"over against all riches."* He has a proper perspective on things. We expect wealth to bring happiness and pleasure into our lives. As such, we put a lot of effort in trying to gain wealth, but the psalmist says that God's testimonies give him much more happiness. Wealth does not warn of the dangers ahead and perhaps even increases those dangers, but the godly person rejoices in the warning signs that he has treasured in his heart. God's Word is of far greater value than all the wealth in the world.

We demonstrate a consecrated resolve (verses 15–16)

1. Determination (verse 15)

   "I will meditate on your precepts." The order of words sometimes indicates the most important element in a sentence. A more literal way of rendering this sentence is, *"In your precepts I will be concerned."* The focus is on God's precepts (military orders, see the comments on verse 4). That is what he is going to be concerned with or meditate upon. He is determined to focus his attention on God's orders.

   He goes on to say he will cause himself to look on God's ways. Is it just a coincidence that the concern of verse 9 has matured from focusing on his own way to being obsessed with God's ways? By determining to be focused on the understanding and application of God's Word, he now finds that his way is not so divergent from God's ways as he might have feared at first.

2. Delight (verse 16)

   The psalmist places God's statutes at the beginning of the sentence, which would literally be rendered, *"In your statutes I shall find myself delighted, I shall not forget Your word."* Those who are opposed to God and His ways try to make us feel as though we are missing out on life if we are devoted to God by following His Word, but the experienced psalm writer says we will find ourselves delighted by being in God's Word. True delight in life comes from being in God's statutes or Word. It is not something we will regret or dread along the way. But the implication is that the godly person makes a determined effort at being delighted in God's statutes. He knows the value of God's Word and the way to true blessedness comes through an adherence to God's Word, so he will make God's Word his delight. He determines not to forget God's Word. He has already made the commitment to treasure God's Word in his heart.

The godly man is rightly concerned with leading a blameless life but realizes the concern must not become an obsession. The obsession is with God and His Word. He resolves that the focus of His attention will be God's Word. He discovers that God's Word is authoritative, a treasure, a cause for joy and worship, a warning sign that causes a person to rejoice, is to be valued more than all wealth, and is the way of delight. I should think that would give us many good reasons to be obsessed with it. Ultimately our obsession provides for the prospect of a blameless life, which God will surely bless.

Psalm 119:17–24 — Gimel

The Prayers of a Godly Man

א

Gimel.

17   Deal bountifully with Your servant,
      That I may live and keep Your word.
18   Open my eyes, that I may behold
      Wonderful things from Your law.
19   I am a stranger in the earth;
      Do not hide Your commandments from me.
20   My soul is crushed with longing
      After Your [judgments] at all times.

21   You rebuke the arrogant, the cursed,
      Who wander from Your commandments.
22   Take away reproach and contempt from me,
      For I observe Your testimonies.
23   Even though princes sit *and* talk against me,
      Your servant meditates on Your statutes.
24   Your testimonies also are my delight;
      They are my counselors.[3]

A godly person has two major concerns in his life: 1) his relationship with God and 2) his relationship with people. This is reflected in what the Lord declares as the two greatest commandments, which

---

[3] *New American Standard Bible: 1995 update.* 1995 (Psalm 119:17–24). LaHabra, CA: The Lockman Foundation.

summarize the whole law. As we study the epistles of the New Testament, we discover that much of the teaching relates to these two areas of concern.

If these are major concerns, then it is reasonable to expect our prayers to relate to them. If we take an honest look at our prayer lives, we would probably find that our prayers primarily focus on our desires, our emotional state, and the needs of those closest to us. It is not wrong to pray for these, but as we grow spiritually our prayers might reflect a greater maturity in how we view our relationship to God vertically and people horizontally.

This paragraph of Psalm 119 begins with a prayer of the psalmist that focuses on his relationship to God and then how his relationship to God affects his relationship to ungodly people. The lesson is that the pursuit of God puts our earthly relationships into perspective.

Our prayers concerning our relationship to God (verses 17–20)
We may be startled that the psalmist, who must be considered a godly man, begins with a cry for God to deal bountifully with him. In asking this, he is pleading for God to be good to him or, as we would say today, that God would bless him. The self-centeredness of this request seems to indicate immaturity in his relationship to God. As we read further, we understand that he makes this request not because he had any special claim, that he was demanding this on the basis of a perceived merit. He was simply begging the favour or grace of God in genuine humility, referring to himself as a servant. He recognizes that he is dependent on God's goodness towards him to experience the fullness of life God had promised. Not only is he dependent on God's goodness to sustain his physical life, but God's goodness is necessary to enjoy life, that he may really live.

The psalmist says that even the ability to keep God's Word is dependent on God's goodness toward him. We live in a world that is so contrary to God's ways that it is difficult to live according to God's Word. That he might live and keep God's Word are not to be seen as two separate results of God's bountiful favour towards him. Rather they are linked by the reality that the continuance and abundance of life is experienced through the close adherence to the Word of God.

As believers in the age of grace, we recognize the need to allow God to define what "bountiful" or "good" means. According to Romans 8:28–29 God's good and perfect gifts for those of us who love Him and are called to accomplish His purposes (do His will) are for the purpose of transforming us into the image of His Son. What the world sees as tragedy is God's goodness to bring about greater maturity and fruitfulness in our lives.

My brother's baby girl was found face down in the swimming pool. She was in a coma for about four months before she slipped into the presence of the Lord. My brother's reflection on that episode in their lives was that even though they would have never wanted this to happen to them, they would not trade the experience away as it brought them so much closer to the Lord and to each other. It deepened their walk with the Lord, which is another way of saying that God had let them experience the life of His Son through the blessing of apparent tragedy. Along with this trial came a renewed search of the scriptures, which helped solidify the truth that God's goodness is always working for our good.

Many people have similar stories to tell, but God's goodness is not always limited to tragedy. Receiving answers to prayer also encourage us to study the Word more diligently, which leads us to a closer walk with the Lord, who promised, *"I came that they may have life, and have it abundantly."* (John 10:10b)

The psalmist also prays for spiritual vision, *"Open my eyes that I may behold wonderful things from Your law"* (verse 18). God's

Word is a treasure house of spiritual truths, and we need God's help to open our eyes to perceive them. The apostle Paul wrote, *"But a natural man does not accept the things of the Spirit of God, for they are foolishness to him: and he cannot understand them, because they are spiritually appraised"* (I Corinthians 2:14). In Ephesians 1:18 he prays, *"that the eyes of your heart may be enlightened...."* The evaluation of God's workings on our behalf can be carried out only with integrity through spiritually opened eyes.

Why does he pray this? In verse 19 he states that he is a stranger on earth and that God should not hide (conceal) the Word from him. God's Word is like a letter from home when we are in a strange environment. The psalmist wants to understand it as well as receive it. Scripture reminds us that as believers we are not at home on this earth. We are pilgrims on a journey to our heavenly home. The pathway is fraught with dangers and hardships, and God's Word is a guide and encouragement along the way. So, like the psalmist, we pray that God would give us spiritual insight and make the Word of God readily available to us.

The psalmist describes the intensity of longing for God's Word as his soul being crushed with the effort and the effort is prolonged (verse 20). Several Psalms speak of an intense longing for God and His Word, but we see so little of that in the lives of Christians. Most churches have reduced their number of services, which means fewer opportunities to hear God's Word being taught and preached. People are not willing to make the effort to expose themselves to more Bible study, so we shut the doors. More and more people are giving up on God and the church because they are not able to discern the "wonderful things" in scripture, so they are not able to perceive God's bountiful care in the bad times as well as the good.

The psalmist's prayer is not for his own wellbeing but that he might have a closer walk with God. He is supremely desirous of a closer relationship to God, which is attained through an obsession with God' Word.

Our prayers concerning our relationship to others (verses 21–24)

We begin with an observation that helps us understand that this prayer is for the psalmist's relationship to those who are ungodly. He observes, *"You [God] rebuke the arrogant, the cursed, who wander from your commandments"* (verse 21). The arrogant person is a presumptuous person who thinks he will not have to answer to God for his actions. Any such person is cursed, meaning he comes under the condemnation of God. Verse 21 says his actions describe one who wanders from God's commandments. In other words, he does not walk in the path laid out by God's Word. The Lord rebukes such a person. We do not know when or how this is manifested, but we do know the certainty of it.

After this preliminary observation, the psalmist makes his request, *"Take away reproach and contempt from me, for I observe your testimonies"* (verse 22). The reproach, or scorn, and contempt come from the arrogant ones of verse 21. His prayer is that God's bountiful care of him (verse 17) is not perceived as God's rebuke because, in contrast to the arrogant person, he observes God's testimonies. For instance, if God determines it is good for him to suffer some hardship or affliction (cf. verses 65–68), and his enemies perceive it to be God's rebuke, then they will heap scorn on him as one who aligns himself with God and suffers the same way they suffer. It was God's will that Jesus be crucified, but He received the mocking scorn of men in His obedience. So, we understand the psalmist to be saying, "Don't treat me as You would an arrogant person" (verse 21). As he studies God's Word, he understands God's ways and responds accordingly. This should prove to be a testimony to the arrogant rather than fodder for the scornful.

Peter expresses this very well in I Peter 3:15–16, *"But sanctify Christ as Lord in your hearts, always being ready to make a defence to everyone who asks you to give an account for the hope that is in you, yet with gentleness and reverence: and keep a good conscience so that in the thing in which you are slandered, those who revile your good behaviour in Christ will be put to shame."*

The reason behind this request seems to be that *"princes sit and talk against me"* (verse 23). If King David is the author of this psalm, he is either talking about his superiors when he was fleeing from King Saul; enemy kings who were trying to bring about his downfall, in which case they are his peers; or Absalom's rebellion. Psalm 3:1–2 says, when David was fleeing from Absalom, *"O Lord, how my adversaries have increased! Many are rising up against me. Many are saying of my soul, 'there is no deliverance for him in God.'"* Whoever these princes are they are significant, and their words are not to be taken lightly.

So, while these princes are sitting and talking against him, the psalmist meditates on God's statutes. Psalm 1:1–2 says, *"How blessed is the man who does not walk in the counsel of the wicked, nor stand in the path of sinners, **nor sit in the seat of the scoffers**! But his delight is in the law of the Lord and in His law he meditates day and night."* [emphasis added] He is not going to follow the counsel of people who wander from God's commands, he does not take their position, and he certainly is not going to pay any heed to their scoffing!

A statute has the underlying significance of words being inscribed on stone and therefore permanent in nature. It needs to be noted that the talk of the princes, who are mere human beings, is short lived, just as they are, in contrast to the statutes of God.

The psalmist goes on to say that God's testimonies are his delight. The word "testimonies" is often found in connection with delight or joy because they are warning signs and reminders of dangers ahead. By paying attention to them we steer clear of danger, and that is something in which to rejoice.

One would expect to get good advice or counsel from princes or rulers. Instead, the psalmist is getting scorn. Never mind, God's testimonies and statutes are his counsellors. They give him guidance and understanding of the true nature of the circumstance.

Daniel in the den of lions is a good example for this portion of the psalm. His contemporaries plotted against him and then spoke against him as Daniel remained faithful in praying to God. What, at first, seemed like the reproach of God when Daniel was thrown into the lions' den turned to a wonderful testimony of God's bountiful care. Daniel's contemporaries experienced the full rebuke of God when they were thrown into the den of lions, who had missed out on a tasty meal.

However, we need to remind ourselves that it doesn't always turn out like it did for Daniel. Even still, we are to have the testimony of Daniel's friends, Shadrach, Meshach, and Abednego in Daniel 3:17–18, *"If it be so, our God whom we serve is able to deliver us from the furnace of blazing fire; and He will deliver us out of your hand, O king.* **But even if He does not, let it be known to you, O king, that we are not going to serve your gods or worship the golden image that you have set up"** (emphasis added). Yes, God did deliver them from the furnace, but they had no assurance that God would do so, and they remained steadfast in the face of what seemed to be certain death. This became a powerful testimony to King Nebuchadnezzar and his court!

Psalm 119:25–32 — Daleth

God's Way and the Life of the Believer

ד

Daleth.

25   My soul cleaves to the dust;
        Revive me according to Your word.
26   I have told of my ways, and You have answered me;
        Teach me Your statutes.

27   Make me understand the way of Your precepts,
        So I will meditate on Your wonders.
28   My soul weeps because of grief;
        Strengthen me according to Your word.
29   Remove the false way from me,
        And graciously grant me Your law.

30   I have chosen the faithful way;
        I have placed Your [judgments] *before me.*
31   I cling to Your testimonies;
        O LORD, do not put me to shame!
32   I shall run the way of Your commandments,
        For You will enlarge my heart.[4]

The value of prayer cannot be overstated, and if prayer is of great value, it would seem reasonable to seek ways to enrich our prayer

---

[4] *New American Standard Bible: 1995 update.* 1995 (Psalm 119:25–32). LaHabra, CA: The Lockman Foundation.

lives. Too often our prayers consist of a long list of our needs and the needs of others. This list of needs ranges from serious health concerns to trivial or selfish desires. We pray for health, for finances, for safety in travel, for the well-being of immediate family and friends, and even for parking spaces at the supermarket.

This section of Psalm 119 will help us perceive needs that are more significant and should be a major focus in our prayers. No, we do not have to stop bringing the whole list before the Lord as we are encouraged to bring everything to our heavenly Father. However, it is in the overcoming of our deepest needs through the application of God's Word and dependency on His Spirit, we begin to experience the abundant life that Jesus promises us in John 10:10. Many of us are missing out on the fullness of life in Christ because we are not addressing the most basic issues in our lives. It is the Lord's intent that we experience His eternal life now! I John 5:11–13 says, *"And the testimony is this, that God has given us eternal life, and this life is in His Son. He who has the Son has the life; he who does not have the Son does not have the life. These things I have written to you who believe in the name of the Son of God, so that you may know that you have eternal life."* This is speaking of our present reality, not our future glorification. This present reality is not just for super saints but for all *"who believe in the name of the Son of God."* The Apostle John definitely has more in mind than just a mental knowledge of a spiritual truth. He wants us to have an experiential knowledge of our eternal life in Christ.

The way of life (verses 25–26)
The second line of verse 25 says, *"revive me."* The Authorized Version says, "quicken Thou me." When I was a teenager, I was, at least in my mother's estimation, more lethargic than the norm. One day in her frustration with me she exclaimed, "Ken, you were born slow and had a relapse!" My slowness has plagued me all my life, but this phrase is not asking for a burst of speed. Neither is it asking for life after experiencing death although it could be applied in an

evangelistic way. The psalmist is a believer in God, so he is not asking for eternal life being convinced that he is dead in his trespasses and sins. When he says, "give me life," he is recognizing that he is not experiencing the fullness of life that should be true of a child of God. In these opening verses of this stanza, he prays concerning two hindrances to experiencing the abundant life.

The first hindrance is his attachment to all that is worldly. *"My soul cleaves to the dust"* does not mean he is literally grovelling in the dust. It is his soul (life) that is stuck to the dust. His vision is earth bound, and the world stimulates his appetite for fleshly and material desires. The wisdom of this world aids him in his pursuit of self-promotion (see I John 2:15–17). As a believer he knows in his heart that what the world presents as hardcore realities are no more than dust or shifting sands. He knows that to be friends with the world is to be God's enemy (see James 4:4). Dust has no value, and it is temporary in that God will destroy the earth with fire. Even though he knows all this, he recognizes that his human (sinful) nature gravitates toward that which is of no value, and in evaluating his life he realizes he does not experience the fullness of life that should be his.

So, he cries out for the very life of God, and he recognizes the answer to that cry for help does not come from the attractions or philosophies of the world but that it always comes according to the Word of God. God's Word has the answer to breaking our bondage to this world, but we need God's help to study, understand, and apply God's Word. With God's help we become obedient students of the book of life and discover an exuberance of life in Christ Jesus.

How many of us are able to discern that this is one of our deepest needs? We are missing out on the life God wants for us because we are so attached to this world. This is not a battle that takes place once in our lifetime and after that we have victory. No, it is a continuing problem, which necessitates an earnestness in prayer for strength to stay away from the shackles of the temporal.

The other problem the psalmist wrestles with is the fickleness of his own heart. Notice the contrast of *"I have told of my ways"* and *"teach me your statutes."* His ways are not God's ways (see Isaiah 55:8–9). His ways are anything but consistent, while God's ways, as found in God's statutes, are fixed, permanent. The psalmist uses the word "statutes" because, as we have already seen, it speaks of permanence (inscribed in stone).

When he declares his ways to God, the next phrase says, *"You have answered me."* Literally it is, *"You have heard me."* In the context of the contrast of his ways to God's statutes, it would appear to make more sense that God heard him in that God understood. This does not mean that God understands and approves but that God understands our fickleness, low mindedness, and deceptiveness. Since God does understand the nature of the human heart, God will certainly respond to a request for instruction in God's statutes.

For some reason we fail to comprehend the seriousness of our whole manner of life being far below the standard of God's nature or glory. If we compare ourselves to those around us, we will certainly not be alarmed, but as we draw closer to God, we begin to see ourselves as a holy God sees us. If we are truly drawing closer to God, we will be horrified at our despicable natures. The abundance of life does not come from conforming to society's standards but to an increasing transformation into the image of Christ through a Spirit-taught heart from the eternal Word of God.

The way of victory (verses 27–29)
The abundant life is a victorious life. According to this portion of the psalm, there are three basic areas in which we need to experience victory.

The first area is the age-old problem of pride. As we look at verse 27, there seems to be an emphasis on an obsession with God's precepts and God's wonders. Orders from a high authority (precepts) are often misunderstood and when misunderstood we resort to complaining. "All these dos and don'ts, rules, regulations, they just want to spoil our fun." The other alternative, which is a more mature and less selfish attitude, is to discern the purpose and reason for them. If they are God's orders, there is a reason for them, and they are for our benefit. The psalmist desires God to help him discern the way of God's precepts.

Next, the psalmist says he wants to meditate on God's wonders as a result of what he has discerned. When we prayerfully seek to discern God's purposes, we will begin to see marvellous and glorious truths about God and His ways. They will be worth pondering for days on end. As the apostle Paul exclaimed as he perceived some glorious truths, *"Oh, the depth of the riches both of the wisdom and knowledge of God! How unsearchable are His judgments and unfathomable His ways!"* (Romans 11:33)

Pride keeps us so focused on ourselves that we miss out on the wonders of God. When we are so full of ourselves, we are full of emptiness, and Jesus came to give us fullness of life! In order to achieve victory over the emptiness of pride, we spend time in our prayer life asking for discernment or understanding of His precepts so that we may focus on His wonders rather than on our worthless attainments.

The second area in which we need victory is in human heartache. We live in a fallen world, and we constantly experience trials and hardships. Without God's support we are hopeless and in despair. The psalmist says, *"his soul weeps with grief"* (verse 28). We are not told of the cause of his grief, and that is not important. We do not need to compare our heartaches with one another. It is enough to know that every person experiences heartache some time or other, and some live many years with heartache with no hope of a solution. This may be what the psalmist is talking about here. So, he prays that God would strengthen him according to the Word of God. He is not referring to the use of the Bible as a magical incantation or a psychological pep pill. Some think their spirits will be lifted just by quoting certain verses, like Psalm 23 or the Lord 's Prayer. The psalmist recognizes that the strength of God for the trials of life can only come in accordance with the teaching of God's Word. It assumes a deep understanding and the ability (by God's Spirit) to apply that teaching. Once we do that, we begin to experience the hope that is found in our faith in Christ.

The trouble with many of us is that we do not have sufficient confidence in the truths of scripture to sustain us in our battle with heartache, discouragement, and even depression. Sometimes the Bible prescribes the forsaking of a particular sin, and in our refusal to repent our souls weep and melt away with no strength to endure. Sometimes the Bible tells us to resolve a relationship conflict, but we are too afraid to rock the boat, and the situation steadily gets worse. Sometimes the Bible speaks to us about the idols in our lives, that God does not have first place, or it alerts us to an attitude that does not appropriate the full forgiveness of sins that was won on the cross. No matter what is required of us, we do not have to go it alone, the Spirit of God gives us the encouragement and ability to do what needs to be done.

Nothing is said here that the cause of the grief will be taken away, but that God will give strength as we adhere to His Word. Some situations will not be resolved in this lifetime, but as God told the apostle Paul, *"My grace is sufficient for you, for power is perfected in weakness"* (II Corinthians 12:9). Through that power of God in the most grievous of hardships, we will experience the abundant, eternal life of Christ!

The final area in which we need victory is that of deceit: *"Remove the false way from me"* (verse 29). Is the psalmist referring to the deceptiveness of his own heart or to the reality that we live in the realm of deceitfulness? The former certainly is true, and it is the constant prayer of every godly person that falsehood and deception would not be part of his life. However, the latter is also a trial and a burden to the sincere follower of Christ. The prayer would be that he would be able to live above the mire of deceitfulness, which characterizes the world of men. The only remedy for this is to embrace God's laws, which are truth. It is a gracious gift of God to have His law in place of the deceitful standards of men and even our own hearts.

We have such deep spiritual needs. We are attached to the attractions and philosophies of this world. We struggle with our own untrustworthiness. We are so fickle! We battle with pride, heartache, and deceitfulness constantly. Yet, we pray endlessly for our needs that Jesus promised to provide in Matthew 6:25–34. The lack of an abundant life is not due to our lack of needs. It is due to our failure to deal earnestly with issues of the heart that rob us of experiencing the fullness of God.

The way of truth (verses 30–32)
The abundance of life can never be at the expense of truth. Jesus is the way, the truth, and the life. When truth is lacking, life loses all its meaning. God's Word is truth, and therefore we are to respond to it in an appropriate manner.

In verse 30 the psalmist says he makes a deliberate choice to follow the faithful or trustworthy way, and in so doing he has placed God's judgments (NASB: "ordinances") before him. Those familiar with a parliamentary system of government understand how present-day judgments are based on historical precedents. God's historical judgments serve as a guide for present-day decisions. The picture of a traveller planning a journey comes to mind as he chooses the route he is going to follow and places the map before him as he charts his course. A modern way of looking at this is the psalmist placing the GPS with the map app of his choice on the dash of his car. In other words, he is not "flying by the seat of his pants." He knows his objective, follows the route to take, and is firmly settled on it.

Then the psalmist says he clings to God's testimonies (verse 31). Once he has chosen the correct map and course, he sticks to it. It does not do him any good to keep changing his mind. An unstable person is a person with no faith according to James 1:5–6. Now he clings to God's testimonies rather than to the dust of verse 25. He is already experiencing victory in his life! Clinging to God's testimonies means he is paying attention to the warning signs and the testimonies of those who have gone before him on the same journey. As long as he stays on course, he has complete confidence that God will not let him down and cause him to suffer shame. There is no shame in following God's testimonies.

Once the decision is made, he runs with it (verse 32). He is devoted to the plan of action and confidence in the plan. Anytime we are devoted to something in which we have confidence, we experience a sense of well-being. However, if the plan is not a reliable plan, or route, the sense of well-being will crumble with the first failure to meet one of our deepest needs. Only the Bible has the answers to our deepest needs, and when those are met, we begin to experience the grandness of life through His Son.

Psalm 119:33–40 — He

Causal Clauses of Commitment

ה

He.

33 Teach me, O LORD, the way of Your statutes,
And I shall observe it to the end.
34 Give me understanding, that I may observe Your law
And keep it with all *my* heart.
35 Make me walk in the path of Your commandments,
For I delight in it.

36 Incline my heart to Your testimonies
And not to *dishonest* gain.
37 Turn away my eyes from looking at vanity,
And revive me in Your ways.
38 Establish Your word to Your servant,
As that which produces reverence for You.
39 Turn away my reproach which I dread,
For Your [judgments] are good.

40 Behold, I long for Your precepts;
Revive me through Your righteousness.[5]

In composing this psalm, the author demonstrates his artistic abilities by making it an acrostic poem. The psalm has twenty-two

---

[5] *New American Standard Bible: 1995 update*. 1995 (Psalm 119:33–40). LaHabra, CA: The Lockman Foundation.

stanzas corresponding to the number of letters in the Hebrew alphabet. Every stanza has eight couplets, or verses, and each couplet begins with the same letter of the alphabet. The first stanza is called "aleph" because aleph is the first letter of the Hebrew alphabet, and each couplet in the stanza starts with aleph.

When a preacher is a slave to alliteration in his sermons, he often runs into difficulty finding a known word that starts with the right letter. The psalmist might have had a struggle or two from time to time as he sought the right word in order to keep up with the acrostic structure of his psalm. Remember, he would not have had access to a thesaurus back then. However, this portion where every word starts with the letter "he" (pronounced "hay") might have been one of his easier sections. In Hebrew the definite article for a noun is "he," and that would have been fairly simple. Also, there are several verb stems that require the verb to start with a "he," and that is what the author uses here. He has chosen a verbal stem (*hiphil*) in the imperative (command) that requires an initial "he." This verbal stem is literally translated as a causative. A causative command, for example, would sound like this, "Cause me to see."

For seven verses, the psalmist uses this verbal form as he asks God to aid him in his walk of commitment to God, and that is the basis for the title of this stanza of Psalm 119. God can aid our commitment to Christ, and removing our attention from God can hinder our commitment. The fortieth verse is a declaration of the psalmist's commitment based upon his heart attitude in the requests he made in the preceding seven verses.

Causes for obedience (verses 33–35)

"Teach me, O Lord, the way of your statutes" (verse 33). The root idea of the word "teach" is to throw or shoot something with the one doing the action having enough control to optimize the aim. In a causative form, it would be rendered literally as, "Cause the way of your statues to be thrown my way." The obvious implication is

that he is requesting the covenant-keeping God, who gave the statutes to Israel in the first place, to teach him.

Ignorance of the covenantal provisions of the agreement is not an excuse for failure in carrying them out. It is important to know them to abide by them. Therefore, the psalmist is asking that the author of the covenant to teach him so that he would have a greater assurance in knowing what the requirements are.

His statement of commitment is that he would keep the statutes forever. He says nothing about understanding, only that he knows what the statutes are that he needs to obey. God gave them, and we are obligated to obey them. Therefore, we depend on God to teach them so that we can be obedient to Him. It seems reasonable to think that God would delight in hearing a request and a commitment such as this.

Then he prays, *"Give me understanding"* (verse 34). Literally it would be "cause me to understand." Notice he has committed himself to obedience even before he understands the covenantal law of God. Our tendency is to want to understand fully before we make any commitment. The agreement to obey is based on the authority of the Lawgiver rather than
our understanding.

His request for understanding is so he may be more fully devoted to keeping God's law. He desires to keep it with all his heart. No half-hearted obedience will suffice. This is another indication of his devotion to God.

Finally, he requests, *"Make me walk in the path of your commandment"* (verse 35). By now you get the idea, "cause me to walk...." No matter the level of commitment, the propensity for failure looms large in the heart of the godliest of persons.

Our intentions may be strong, but we still have to depend on divine enablement.

The reason he requests this puts him on a higher level than most of us will ever achieve, *"for I delight in it."* The apostle Paul expressed the struggle very well in Romans 7:21-23, *"I find then the principle that evil is present in me, the one who wants to do good. For I joyfully concur with the law of God in the inner man, but I see a different law in the members of my body, waging war against the law of my mind and making me a prisoner of the law of sin which is in my members."* Hopefully, as we grow in our walk with the Lord we will come to a place where His ways are a delight, but even then, we will not be relieved from the struggle with sin. Sin is pleasurable; otherwise we would not be tempted to sin. After we evaluate competing claims about what is delightful, we look to the Lord to help us walk in His ways rather than the pleasures of sin.

Notice the progression of thought, our commitment is based on the authority of the Lawgiver, and we depend on Him to teach us His law. Our commitment is enhanced by an understanding of God's law that He gives us, and our commitment is a delight rather than a burden, but we need God's enablement to keep that commitment.

Causes for disobedience (verses 36–39)
It really does not surprise us that the psalmist finds obstacles to obedience. After all, our adversary, the devil, is not going to make it easy for us to follow through in our commitment to Christ.

The first obstacle is an obvious one, money (verse 36). My rendition of this verse is, *"Cause my heart to incline towards Your warning signs and not to illegal profit."* The Bible does not say that money itself or that earning money is wrong. I Timothy 6:10 warns us that it is the love of money for which we have to be on the alert. There are many warnings in scripture about obsessing over money as that will lead to wrong behaviour, chief of which is diminishing loyalty to Christ. The tenth commandment is somewhat of a summary command for the last five as it prohibits coveting of anything. The coveting of money can lead to illegal activity depending on the level of obsession. The psalmist wants God to help him be obsessed with God's testimonies rather than that which would lead to criminal behaviour.

Closely related to the previous request is the psalmist's prayer, *"Cause my eyes to pass rapidly from worthless things"* (verse 37). We are tempted through the eye gate because objects that are harmful to our spiritual lives are attractive in nature. The psalmist is praying that his eyes would pass on rapidly when he saw something alluring but harmful. We are not to focus on or let our gaze linger on the harmful object. Eve, apparently, took too long a look at the forbidden fruit and brought trouble on all mankind (Genesis 3:6).

The allurement of harmful things is the inherent promise of enjoyment and more pleasure in our lives. Notice the psalmist calls them worthless things, or vanity. This is a word used for idols. The reality is emptiness, and the promise is never realized. The pursuit of anything at the expense of a walk with the living God is an idolatrous pursuit, which leaves the pursuer empty. The psalmist recognizes the fullness of life comes not from the pursuit of worthless idols but the adherence to the ways of God.

When the psalmist cries out, *"Cause Your word to be established to Your servant"* (verse 38), he is imploring God to fix His Word firmly in its performance and in his mind. It is God's Word that produces the fear or reverence of the Lord. Whenever a doubt creeps into our thinking, whether it is because of a set of circumstances or because of a misunderstanding of the scriptures, our fear of the Lord slackens. The psalmist's prayer is that God would remove any doubt that would cause him to lose his fear of the Lord, which is the beginning of true wisdom.

Lastly, he says, *"Cause my reproach (disgrace) to pass rapidly from me"* (verse 38). No one likes scorn or disgrace, whatever may be the cause of it, and it can be a hindrance to our commitment to follow God. The meaning of this verse may be as follows, "Since I know your judgments are good (whatever God judicially decides for me) do not let me forsake them due to fear, or dread, of disgrace or reproach." It would appear the psalmist is not asking to have the reproach removed. Rather he is asking that it may not linger inordinately, and, as a servant, he is submissive to God's will for him. Christ is our ultimate example in this. It was God the Father's judgment that Jesus should bear the reproach of men and go to the cross. The agony in Jesus' heart as he contemplated the horror of what faced Him is best understood in the gloom of the Garden of Gethsemane. But He did not turn from following God's will for Him.

So, we have discovered four hindrances that can keep us from being faithful to God: 1) the love of money, 2) the pursuit of the worthless, 3) the danger of doubt, and 4) the dread of reproach. May God give us an inclination to His testimonies, cause our eyes to turn away from worthless objects of affection, fix His Word in our hearts, and cause the reproach we face in being His followers to pass on rapidly even though we accept it from Him.

Causes for eternal life (verse 40)
The psalmist pleads, *"Behold, I long for your precepts."* Or "Lord, look at my heart carefully. I long for your authoritative orders." The evidence for this is the series of requests made in the previous seven verses. He wants to learn, understand, and be obedient to God's Word. He wants anything that might be a hindrance to his obedience to be removed and he knows only God can give him the victory. If we want the fullness of life that Jesus offers us, then we must do our part in being totally committed to obedience.

So, his last prayer in this paragraph is that God would give him life. As we have explained before, this is the abundant life, which is nothing less than the eternal life of God experienced through the new birth during this lifetime! Galatians 2:20 says, *"I have been crucified with Christ; and it is no longer I who live, but Christ lives in me; and the life which I now live in the flesh I live by faith in the Son of God, who loved me and gave Himself up for me."*

For us to experience the eternal life of Christ right now, we have to be absolutely committed, and God's part, other than salvation, is to give us the fullness of the experience of that life. Even if we are not experiencing the eternal life of Christ does not mean that we do not have it. Having eternal life is a gift of God that we receive by faith. Experiencing that eternal life is the blessing of fellowship with our Saviour. May we long for more than just having eternal life and do what is necessary, with God's help, to experience eternal life.

Psalm 119:41–48 — Vav

Prayers and Promises

I

Vav.

41   May Your lovingkindnesses also come to me, O LORD,
Your salvation according to Your word;

42   So I will have an answer for him who reproaches me,
For I trust in Your word.

43   And do not take the word of truth utterly out of my
mouth,
For I wait for Your [judgments].

44   So I will keep Your law continually,
Forever and ever.

45   And I will walk at liberty,
For I seek Your precepts.

46   I will also speak of Your testimonies before kings
And shall not be ashamed.

47   I shall delight in Your commandments,
Which I love.

48   And I shall lift up my hands to Your commandments,
Which I love;
And I will meditate on Your statutes.[6]

---

[6] *New American Standard Bible: 1995 update*. 1995 (Psalm 119:41–48). LaHabra, CA: The Lockman Foundation.

To be called a pious person is not always a compliment. It is often associated with pride and hypocrisy. However, it is a good word to describe a person who sincerely expresses devotion to God, which might be evident in his zealous prayers or acts of worship and ministry. Therefore, it is appropriate to describe this section of Psalm 119 as "The Prayers and Promises of a Pious Man." (It also has nice alliteration!)

Again, the psalmist would have had an easier time working out the acrostic for this section because the Hebrew letter "vav" is attached to the first word of most sentences and simply means "and, also, or so." If you have a fairly literal translation of the Bible, you will notice that most of the sentences in both the narrative and the poetic sections begin with "and."

The psalmist was clearly a pious man, and we benefit from observing how he prays and the commitments he makes with the intent that we emulate his behaviour.

A prayer for God's lovingkindnesses (verses 41–42)
In keeping with the nature of Hebrew poetry, it is clear the psalmist specifically wants God's salvation as God's act of lovingkindness toward him. The salvation mentioned here is probably related to the deliverance he sought from the affliction he was experiencing from his enemies. This affliction appears repeatedly in this psalm, and it is evidently quite severe.

Whether one seeks eternal salvation or relief from affliction, it is always based on God's lovingkindnesses. Titus 3:5–6 reads, *"He saved us, not on the basis of deeds which we have done in righteousness, but according to His mercy (lovingkindness), by the washing of regeneration and renewal of the Holy Spirit, whom He poured out upon us richly through Jesus Christ our Savior."*

Notice it is God's salvation/deliverance. The psalmist rejects the notion that he is dependent on his own ingenuity or on another's aid. The Israelites in the Old Testament are repeatedly warned against looking to human help whenever they found themselves in difficulty. True faith would have us look only to God for His help whenever we find ourselves in a tight spot. God's deliverance is always an act of lovingkindness/mercy and can never be demanded, bribed, or earned.

Also, God's deliverance is according to His Word/promise. God will never violate His Word in order to do us a favour. James 4:3 reminds us, *"You ask and do not receive, because you ask with wrong motives, so that you may spend it on your pleasures."* God takes note of our motives, and if our request does not promote the glory of God, He may not pay attention to our request.

Now the psalmist introduces us to the difficulty he is experiencing. He does not identify those who are reproaching him, nor does he reveal the specifics of their reproach. Throughout the psalm we can understand that these enemies were afflicting him so severely that he felt he would lose his life. If God would deliver him, he would have an answer for these opponents. His request for deliverance is not for the satisfaction of outwitting his enemies; it is based on his absolute trust in God's Word. God's deliverance is according to His promise, and therefore the deliverance may not come in the form we expect. When that is the case, we must demonstrate complete confidence in God's Word as it is the truth and transcends our expectations and thoughts.

If we do not have full confidence/trust in God's Word, we will have doubts about our eternal salvation (the most significant deliverance of God); we will have doubts about God being merciful and loving; and we will have no authoritative answer for those who reproach or taunt us.

Let us learn from the psalmist how we are to pray for God's help:

1. We do not deserve God's help; God gives it because He is merciful and loving.
2. God will answer in accordance with His promise (Word). We can claim the promise from the Bible that relates specifically to our situation.
3. Overcoming the problem is not the primary objective. The primary objective is for an increasing measure of personal confidence in God's Word.

A prayer for the availability of God's Word (verses 43–46)

Literally this reads, *"And do not snatch away from my mouth the word of truth to an overwhelming degree."* If, as he said in verse 42, his confidence is in God's Word, then it follows that God's Word is his hope in which he waits. Without the Word of God, we have nothing in which to hope. *"We are of all men most to be pitied"* (I Corinthians 15:19) speaking of our hope in the resurrection. The gentiles are described as *"having no hope and without God in this world"* (Ephesians 2:12). That is a pitiful condition to be in.

Therefore, it is the psalmist's request in prayer that God would not allow the complete and irrevocable removal of God's Word from him. How can that be accomplished? It might be the result of a law passed by a government opposed to the gospel or being taken prisoner and removed from all contact with the outside world. It could be the result of blindness or deafness. But more than all of these, it might be a reference to his facility to use the Word that is treasured in his heart (verse 11) as he defends himself before his enemies, or that his memory is in some way impaired so that he cannot speak of his hope or bring the Word to mind to strengthen his hope in the midst of dire circumstances.

What a tragedy for a pious person to lose the facility to access the Word of God either by memory or by some external source. It is our confidence and hope. Without it we are truly empty.

If the Lord answers this request, the psalmist can confidently proclaim he will keep God's Law continually. By using the term "Law" he is referring to the "Torah," which is God's covenant with Israel. God's covenant is a most solemn agreement that He has made with His people, Israel. It is inconceivable that God would ever violate His covenantal Law, so the psalmist reciprocates by claiming his fidelity to that Law as a day-by-day way of life. He keeps the Law through carefully observing (studying) the Law with the intent of doing what it says.

With that kind of expectation, the psalmist has the confidence to *"walk at liberty"* as he seeks (examines carefully) God's precepts. The precepts are precise orders given by a higher authority. In terms of the Bible, the authority is no less than God. There is no higher authority. God's Word is precise and clear. A person who is devoted to God will carefully examine the authoritative Word of God with the purpose of utmost obedience.

The irony is the psalmist has found that following God's orders is not restrictive, as doubters would have us believe, but is very liberating. We have great liberty within the clearly identifiable boundaries. Unclear boundaries are restrictive, and outside the boundaries are pitfalls and dangers that cause us to tread carefully. The liberty within the clear boundaries gives us the confidence to live our life to the fullest.

He also has confidence to speak of God's testimonies before kings. Testimonies, as we have already noted, act as warning signs. Is the psalmist King David speaking about testifying before his peers? Sometimes our peers are the hardest to witness to or warn of God's judgment against sin. Maybe the psalmist is an ordinary person, like we are, and he is expressing his confidence of speaking the authoritative precepts of God to those in authority.

With the Word of God confidently on our lips, we have great liberty knowing He will approve of us if we observe his commands. Also, with the same confidence, we are able to speak bravely before anyone because it is not our idea but God's Word that is the source of our communication.

Whenever Larry King (the famous talk show host of CNN, now deceased) interviewed known Christian leaders, he would almost always ask the question, "Surely you don't think that God will send anyone to hell that isn't a Christian? How can you be so closed minded?" Those interviewed would either squirm uncomfortably or give an evasive reply like, "I will let God judge. I cannot take the place of God." The trouble with that answer is that God has already told us how He will judge. Thinking how I would answer, I have come up with this: "It is not dependent on what I think but on what God has said in His Bible. Yes, I believe the Bible, and what the Bible says matters more than what I want to believe, think, or say." Larry King's question is simply a question of whether one believes the Bible. He phrases it in such a way that it makes the person look as if it was his idea that people go to hell. I have nothing to fear when I say what the Bible affirms, and the rejection I may experience is not of me but of the Word of God.

Three promises concerning God's Word (verses 47–48)
We can expect the psalmist to be brimming with enthusiasm for God and His Word. He makes three promises that are rooted in the totality of our human personality.

1. *"I shall delight myself in Your commandments."* Literally it reads, *"I shall find myself delighted in Your commandments."* This is not an unexpected experience but a determination to be delighted in God's commandments.

There is no sense of, "I am going to enjoy this, even if it kills me." The reason for his determination to be delighted is because he loves God's Word. My soul delights in what I love. If a person is not delighted in the Word of God, he cannot claim a love for God's Word. This is a commitment of his <u>emotions</u>.

2. *"I shall lift up my hands to Your commands."* Hands speaks of doing (activity). The psalmist is expressing his commitment to do what God commands. The motive, once again, is his love for God's commands. This is a commitment of the <u>will</u>.

3. *"I will meditate on Your statutes."* Here he is engaging his intellect to the careful consideration of what God's Word says. This is a commitment of the <u>intellect</u>.

God demands our total being to be in surrender to His will. To be emotional in worship without a commitment to obedience is one of the worst forms of hypocrisy. Obedience without the emotion of joy is servitude. The study of the Word for personal amusement, lacking in joy and obedience, is lifeless and results in eternal loss.

A pious person devoted to God seeks God's merciful help in times of need. He trusts God to help him have the facility to speak God's Word in every situation. He also engages his whole human personality to the assimilation of God's Word in his walk with the Lord.

That kind of a pious person is what we should all strive to be like!

Psalm 119:49–56 — Zayin

The Word of God Changes Us

ז

Zayin.

49	Remember the word to Your servant, In which You have made me hope.
50	This is my comfort in my affliction, That Your word has revived me.
51	The arrogant utterly deride me, *Yet* I do not turn aside from Your law.
52	I have remembered Your [judgments] from of old, O LORD, And comfort myself.
53	Burning indignation has seized me because of the wicked, Who forsake Your law.
54	Your statutes are my songs In the house of my pilgrimage.
55	O LORD, I remember Your name in the night, And keep Your law.
56	This has become mine, That I observe Your precepts.[7]

Most of us have heard the old joke about how churches of various denominations would meet the challenging need of changing a burnt-out light bulb in the building. Since I am not ashamed to be

---

[7] *New American Standard Bible: 1995 update*. 1995 (Psalm 119:49–56). LaHabra, CA: The Lockman Foundation.

called a Baptist, I will give the Baptist church account on how to change a light bulb: *"CHANGE?"* The shock that something needs to be changed is not limited to Baptists; I am fairly sure of that. We've all heard the response, "We've always done it this way!" or "If it ain't broke, don't fix it!"

The problem is, we are "broke" because of sin, and we do need to be fixed. Only the Holy Spirit is able to change a life, but He uses the Word of God in our lives to bring about that change. The Bible has to be more than a dusty book on a shelf or even a much-read book for curiosity's sake. The psalmist of Psalm 1 writes, speaking of the godly man, *"But his delight is in the law of the Lord and in His law he meditates day and night."* In Psalm 119:11 we read, *"Your word I have treasured in my heart,"* then notice the change expected from this, *"that I may not sin against You."* It is a simple truth; the internalized Word of God changes us.

When God acts upon His Word, we experience hope (verses 49–52)

When the psalmist prays for God to "remember" His Word, he is not assuming that God has forgotten what He has said. This is an expression found frequently in the Old Testament as an idiom meaning the person who does the remembering is about to act on behalf of someone. After Noah and his family had been in the ark for many days, we read in Genesis 8:1, *"but God remembered Noah."* God never forgot Noah, but at this point in the narrative, He is going to start acting in a new way on behalf of Noah.

Similarly, in Genesis 30:22 we read, *"Then God remembered Rachel."* Rachel, the second wife of Jacob, had been barren, but now God allows her to conceive. The same idea is found in I Samuel 1:19 as God gives Hannah a child in answer to her prayers.

We also see this in the New Testament. One of the thieves crucified with Jesus cries out, *"Jesus, remember me when You come into Your kingdom!"* I am sure the thief was hoping for a lot more than Jesus remembering him from heaven, "Oh yes, I remember you, you died on the cross next to mine. How is it down there? A little too warm for you?"

So, our psalmist pleads with God to begin acting on the Word given to him. As he claims to be a servant, we can safely assume he is not demanding this but simply pleading for God to help him with his need according to God's own Word to His servant. The psalmist has placed his hope in God's Word and therefore claims that God is the author of his hope.

If the psalmist is David (prior to his reign as king), he might be referring to his anointing to be king of Israel (I Samuel 16:13) while he was fleeing for his life from either Saul or the Philistines. Or, perhaps when he was on the run from his own son, Absalom, he asked God to act upon the Word God had given him in II Samuel 7:4–11, which we call the Davidic Covenant.

Anyone who believes God's Word to be true can make his request to God based on that Word. Those of us who are not Jewish are reminded of the description of salvation for the Gentiles in Ephesians 2:11–22. This passage states that we, before salvation, were *"far off,"* *"having no hope,"* and *"without God."* Jesus, by His death on the cross, has brought us *"near,"* and we have access to God! I Peter 3:15 speaks of the *"hope that is in you."* I Thessalonians 4:13 says that because we have the hope of being with Jesus one day, we are not to *"grieve as do the rest who have no hope."* God Himself has given us hope through His Word, and we can pray that God will act upon His Word so that our hope does not diminish over time.

This hope (verse 49) is displayed in the comfort the psalmist experiences. First, it comforts him when he is afflicted (verse 50). It is the promises of God that comfort him, and that comfort revives his spirit. He is probably not referring to impending death but that, whatever his afflictions were, he derived comfort from God's promises, and that gave him a new zest for life. The internalized Word of God changes us in the way we react to affliction or adversity.

Instead of getting discouraged or even depressed, we seek comfort from the Word of God and that revives our spirit.

Meditate on some of the promises of God:

> John 14:18, *"I will not leave you as orphans; I will come to you."* Yes, Jesus spoke this to His disciples, but the promise is fulfilled in all of us by the indwelling of the Holy Spirit from salvation onward. We are not orphans!

> John 16:33, *"These things I have spoken to you, so that in Me you may have peace. In the world you will have tribulation, but take courage; I have overcome the world."*

> James 1:18, *"In the exercise of His will He brought us forth by the word of truth so that we would be a kind of first fruits among His creatures."*

> I Peter 1:23, *"For you have been born again not of seed which is perishable but imperishable, that is, the living and enduring word of God."* It is by the Word of God that we have spiritual life, and that spiritual life gives us comfort and hope as we cope with the hardships in this life.

> Romans 8:16-18, *"The Spirit Himself testifies with our spirit that we are children of God, and if children, heirs also, heirs of God and fellow heirs with Christ, if indeed we suffer with Him so that we may also be glorified with Him. For I consider that the sufferings of this present time are not worthy to be compared with the glory that is to be revealed to us."* What

hope those verses cause to spring up in our hearts as we go through adversity!

Not only does the Word offer comfort in the midst of affliction, but it also gives comfort when we are ridiculed. The text says, *"The arrogant utterly deride me."* A little mocking and ridicule are more than just a bit bothersome, but when they become unbearable from their ceaseless persistence, we begin to lose hope. We see no way out. The psalmist says that during all this, he does not turn from God's law. When we resort to God's Word and commit ourselves to it, we find it is the one recourse that offers real hope in a hopeless situation.

His comfort comes especially from the reminders of God's judgments of old. The enduring stories of old that recount the judgments of God are great sources of comfort. The God who sent the flood to punish the wicked but saved Noah, a righteous man; the God who parted the Red Sea to give His people safe passage but then destroyed the pursuing Egyptian army; the God who drove out the immoral Canaanites so that His people could possess the promised land—He is the same God who has chosen us to be His children through faith in Jesus, the Son of God. God does not change and will watch over us and scoff at those who shake their fists at Him (Psalm 2:4).

So, there are at least two benefits from internalizing the Word of God for our comfort through hope: 1) God always keeps His promises so that we do not need to despair when facing hardships, and 2) The examples of the judgments of an unchanging God found in His Word on behalf of His people give us great comfort and assurance. The word "hope" in verse 49 means confident or assured expectations. The change wrought in our hearts through the application of the Word of God is one of comfort and assurance in the face of affliction or ridicule.

When we act upon His Word, we exhibit Christlikeness (verses 53–56)

Verse 56 is the reason for the changes in our character found in verses 53–55. The psalmist states, *"This has become mine, that (because) I observe Your precepts."* "This" refers to the observations found in the preceding three verses. To the best of his ability he has observed God's precepts, His precise and authoritative orders.

1. The observed word produces a horror of sin (verse 53). Our text captures it best by calling it *"burning indignation."* It could be rendered as raging heat. How horrified are we by sin in general, especially when it occurs among God's people? It seems as we draw closer to the time of Christ's return, we become less bothered by the prevalence of sin, even in the church. Could it be that we are not as devoted to the study, assimilation, and application of the Word as we need to be? Even Lot was greatly disturbed by the wicked lifestyle of the people of Sodom, and though he was not exactly a spiritual giant, he was called a righteous man (2 Peter 2:7–8). It would appear there was enough righteousness in him that he recoiled at their sin, though not enough to leave that place.

   Can you imagine what it was like for Christ to become a man and live in this sin- corrupted world? His rage in the temple must have been something to behold! If we are truly devoted to the careful obedience of the Word of God, we will become more like Christ in our abhorrence of sin.

2. The Word kept produces joy (verse 54). A horror of sin keeps us from feeling at home in this world. The psalmist understands this life is just a journey that will

come to an end someday. The world is just a stopping-over place. Living in it is not always easy, and there are pitfalls along the way, but the enduring Word of God (statutes) becomes songs of joy from the heart.

Christlikeness is recognizing *"the joy set before"* us as we endure the cross He has called us to bear, and we despise the shame that comes from being His followers (Hebrews 12:2). The wonder of it all is that He has given us His Word to sustain us (*"Man shall not live on bread alone but on every word that proceeds from the mouth of God,"* Deuteronomy 8:3), and that sustenance is so refreshing and comforting that we break out into songs of joy!

3. The Word kept produces love (verse 55). Bear with me as I might be stretching the interpretation just a tad. What do you think about when you cannot sleep at night? I suppose most of us are so full of our burdens and problems that we wake up disturbed by them. The remedy for that is Philippians 4:6–7, but that is not in the scope of this discussion.

   My wife, Mary, and I were engaged for more than a year. I was in seminary, and Mary, having finished college, was living with her parents more than 1,000 miles away and working. The rare times I would awaken in the middle of the night would be to worry about a paper or exam coming up or to think of my lovely bride to be. I am fairly certain the psalmist was not worrying about his problems as much as he was focusing on God's reputation (name) derived from the Word of God. It occupied his thinking in his sleepless moments and motivated him to keep God's law so he would not tarnish God's reputation. Somehow, in my thinking, this is a demonstration of a deep love for God.

Another consideration is that this is his contemplation when there is no one else around. What he is in public, he is in secret! Jesus said, *"If you keep My commandments, you will abide in My love; just as I have kept My Father's commandments and abide in His love"* (John 15:10). How Christlike are we? Are we abiding in His love secretly as well as outwardly?

The internalized Word of God changes us from fretful worriers, who have no hope, to comforted children of God, who have a confident assurance in His faithfulness as described in the Bible. Also, the internalized Word of God changes us *"from glory to glory"* (II Corinthians 3:18) into the image of Christ. When we grow in our repulsion of sin, we have the joy of the Lord in our hearts as we travel to our heavenly home, and we love God so much we think of how we might enhance His reputation by our obedience to the Bible.

Psalm 119:57–64 — Cheth

A Longing for God's Lovingkindness

ת

Heth.

57 The LORD is my portion;
    I have promised to keep Your words.
58 I sought Your favor with all *my* heart;
    Be gracious to me according to Your word.

59 I considered my ways
    And turned my feet to Your testimonies.
60 I hastened and did not delay
    To keep Your commandments.

61 The cords of the wicked have encircled me,
    But I have not forgotten Your law.
62 At midnight I shall rise to give thanks to You
    Because of Your righteous [judgments].
63 I am a companion of all those who fear You,
    And of those who keep Your precepts.

64 The earth is full of Your lovingkindness, O LORD;
    Teach me Your statutes.[8]

---

[8] *New American Standard Bible: 1995 update*. 1995 (Psalm 119:57–64). La Habra, CA: The Lockman Foundation.

It is natural for us to want God to be gracious to us. We avoid adversity at all cost, and when we do find ourselves in a tight spot, we cry out to God to get us out of the mess. Several years ago, a book was written based on the prayer of Jabez found in I Chronicles 4:9–10, purporting to have found the secret to having a life free from problems. Unfortunately, the account in the Bible is brief, and we are not given much detail concerning the circumstances. We do notice that he was *"more honorable than his brothers,"* but God's Word does not tell us what that means. Given the brevity of the account, we would be better off not making this incident a theological dissertation on getting what we want by praying.

The second line of verse 58 is a prayer for God's grace. However, the psalmist says, *"according to Your word (promise)."* We can never pray for God's grace on our own merits. God will always grant it in keeping with His promise. We have already seen similar requests in verses 17 and 41 of this Psalm. Consequently, we can be assured of two conditions when God would answer favourably: 1) When one desires to enter a right relationship with God as seen in the prayer of the repentant tax collector in Luke 18:13, and 2) When one is already in a right relationship with God and pursues a deeper one. Psalm 119:57–64 give us four types of evidence that the psalmist is pursuing a right relationship with God.

He prays for God's grace (verses 57–58)

First, he declares, *"The Lord is my portion."* The psalmist has in mind the promises God made to the tribe of Levi in Joshua 13:7 and 33 (cf. Numbers 18:20). They did not receive any territory among the tribes of Israel because God was their inheritance, or portion, and the service in the tabernacle was God's special provision for them. In writing Psalm 16, David claims this blessing for himself in verse 5 as one who recognizes that all the material blessings one may attain in this life are nothing compared to fellowship with God.

Jeremiah makes the same claim in Lamentations 3:24. The psalmist captures the essence of finding his full satisfaction in God alone. Jesus told the crowd in the Sermon on the Mount, *"But seek first His kingdom and His righteousness, and all these things shall be added to you"* (Matthew 6:33). Many people devote their lives to pursuing the best this world can offer and leave God as an afterthought. If we really desire God's grace in our lives, we will understand that God is to be our all in all and that He has promised to take care of the rest.

Next, the psalmist makes the Word of God the rule for his life. He promises to keep God's words. Promises to God are not to be made lightly, for God will hold us to them. God does extend His grace to those of us who make it a commitment to keep the Bible as the rule for our lives. Consider the employee who is lazy and undependable asking with temerity for a raise. His employer is not likely to consider his request until he sees some effort and commitment.

Lastly, the psalmist demonstrates that his dependency is on God alone. *"I sought Your favour with all my heart."* Literally the phrase could be rendered, *"I stroke Your face, O God,"* or *"I have sought to make the face of God soft towards me."* His wholehearted commitment to keeping God's Word is to ensure that God was favourably entreated on his behalf. We cannot earn God's favour, but we can be assured that God is pleased when He sees that we are not looking for blessings or favours other than from God. He is the only true source of all blessings.

Having declared that his relationship with the covenant-keeping God is more important to him than anything found in this world, that he has promised to keep God's words, and that with singleness of heart he seeks God's favour, he makes his request that God would be gracious to him. With a heart's devotion like that, we can be assured that God would be delighted to be gracious to us.

He repents of his ways (verses 59–60)

A regular, honest appraisal of oneself is a healthy habit. The psalmist takes a good, long look at where he is going. He considered or calculated his ways, and, apparently, he needed a course adjustment. He turned to the way marked out by God's testimonies. He had not been heeding the warning signs along life's pathway, so he made a conscious choice to turn from his wrong direction to go on the path that God marks out in the Word. We call this repentance. The prodigal son in Luke 15:17–18 illustrates this beautifully, *"But when he came to his senses, he said, 'How many of my father's hired men have more than enough bread, but I am dying here with hunger! I will get up and go to my father....'"* Not only did he make a course correction, but he did it quickly. There was no reluctance. He has made the assessment that his ways were not getting him anywhere, and the path of God's commandments was the better choice.

Repentance is absolutely necessary for salvation, but it is also required for keeping on course. Piloting a ship on the pathless sea, the pilot depends on his navigational instruments. The winds and currents constantly push the ship off course, and the pilot continually brings the great ship back on track. In the same way, the world, the flesh, and the devil lure us off course, but we have the Bible to help us get back on track. Let us not delay in making course corrections for our life's journey.

He exhibits new loyalties (verses 61–63)

We are surrounded by unbelievers, and their ways could easily ensnare us. God does not remove us from the pressures of our culture that are contrary to His ways, but He has given us His Word to guide us and give us strength. Like the psalmist, we may feel trapped, encircled with the ropes of the wicked, but we can follow his example, *"I have not forgotten Your law."* He not only remembers, but he acts in accordance with God's covenantal law. He exhibits loyalty to the Word even though the wicked surround him. When Peter was surrounded by soldiers, onlookers, and servants around a bonfire, he forgot what Jesus had told him and denied his Lord in the pressure of the crowd.

We demonstrate a longing for God's lovingkindness by being loyal to the Lord when we are alone. In the middle of the night, in his sleepless moments when no one else is around, the psalmist thanks God for His righteous judgments. He focuses on God's judgments and is filled with thanksgivings that God's ways are always right and just. When there is no one else around, we can drop the pretence and be ourselves. Are we as spiritual in secret as we are in front of others?

"A man is known by the company he keeps" is a well-known saying. If we really desire God's lovingkindness in our lives, we will exhibit a loyalty to those who also love the Lord. These are characterized by a fear of the Lord and keeping God's precepts as a result of their fear of the Lord. Those who recognize God's Word is derived from the highest of all authorities will endeavour to obey it. The psalmist says these are his friends or companions. If a Christian finds he has more in common with unbelievers than with fellow Christians, he cannot be serious about longing for God's lovingkindness. God extends His favour to the company of the righteous. It follows that faithful church attendance is an indicator of one's loyalty to other believers.

He perceives God's lovingkindness (verse 64)
A person who is walking in fellowship with God as described in these verses, not only desires God's favour, but he will also begin to see that His lovingkindness is evident everywhere. The discovery of God's lovingkindness is so astounding that the psalmist cries out for God to teach him more. He wants God to teach him His statutes. The more we learn from God's sure, abiding Word, the more we will be able to discern God's grace and mercy in every area of our lives.

If we are longing for God's lovingkindness in our lives, we will be satisfied in and depend on God alone, and we will be committed to His Word alone. We will take a good look at our ways and see that they are not in keeping with God's ways. We will then quickly turn from our ways and turn towards the way of God's testimonies. We will remain loyal to God's Word when pressured by the crowd. Even in our private, contemplative moments, we will be loyal to the Lord in our thoughts. Our loyalty extends to fellow believers, especially to our church. Then the Lord will open our eyes to all His wondrous blessings that surround us. Without a deep commitment to the Word of God, we will be unaware of all that God does for us every day.

Psalm 119:65–72 — Teth

God is Good

ט

Teth.

65   You have dealt well with Your servant,
           O LORD, according to Your word.
66   Teach me good discernment and knowledge,
           For I believe in Your commandments.
67   Before I was afflicted I went astray,
           But now I keep Your word.
68   You are good and do good;
           Teach me Your statutes.

69   The arrogant have forged a lie against me;
           With all *my* heart I will observe Your precepts.
70   Their heart is covered with fat,
           But I delight in Your law.
71   It is good for me that I was afflicted,
           That I may learn Your statutes.
72   The law of Your mouth is better to me
           Than thousands of gold and silver *pieces*.[9]

A verse that has comforted us in times of adversity is Romans 8:28, *"and we know that God causes all things to work together for good to those who love God, to those who are called according to His*

---

[9] *New American Standard Bible: 1995 update*. 1995 (Psalm 119:65–72). La Habra, CA: The Lockman Foundation.

purpose." God saved us to bring Himself glory, and He orchestrates everything in our lives towards that end. There are no mistakes with God. Romans 8:29 tells us He predestined us to be conformed to the image of His Son. We who were dead in our trespasses and sins, utterly corrupt, and at enmity with God, He saved so we could become like Jesus, which always glorifies Him.

We don't mind when life is treating us well, but in the good times it is easy for us to be satisfied with the status quo instead of progressing in holiness. God allows adversity in our lives to continue the process of sanctification. However, adversity alone is not sufficient to accomplish God's purpose for us. We need to be immersed in the Word of God. Our portion of Psalm 119 teaches us that God uses affliction to teach us the value of His Word.

We evaluate the many facets of God's goodness (verses 65–68)

Previously, the psalmist requested that God be good to him and treat him favourably (verses 17, 41, 58). Now he states as a matter of fact that God is good to him. This may be an indication that he is maturing in his walk with God. The word "good" (or variations in English) is found throughout these verses (65–66, 68, 71–72).

As he considers the circumstances of his life, he is able to discern that the Lord is always good because the Lord always acts according to His Word. This is especially meaningful as the Lord is the one who inaugurated the covenant with His people, and He, as God, will never fail to keep the obligations that pertain to Him. The Lord (Yahweh) is the name that reminds Israel that God is a personal being who has revealed Himself to them and enters a covenant relationship with them. The psalmist evaluates the circumstances in his life in light of the Word of Yahweh and declares that the Lord has done well with him. The Lord can never violate His Word.

We describe some men with the statement, "He's as good as his word." This means that such a person is known for his integrity. A mere human can never know the end from the beginning in any circumstance and may utter some promise that would be impossible for him to keep. We are understanding enough to forgive him due to circumstances beyond his control and still maintain that he is a man of his word. However, God knows everything, the end from the beginning, and He is the one who orchestrates all events to bring about the very things He has purposed and spoken. We never have to make excuses for God!

Though we have the Word of the Lord, it is not always easy to understand His ways in our lives. The psalmist prays for discernment and knowledge, asking that the Lord Himself would teach him. The word "discernment" literally means to taste or to test by tasting. It is learning by experience. If the Lord never allows us to experience hardship, we will miss the delight of tasting God's goodness. The word "knowledge" means to know thoroughly. Not only do we need a taste of God's goodness, but we also need to gain a deeper insight into His character and ways. It is a prayer to know the Lord more intimately. The reason for this prayer is the psalmist believes in the Lord's commandments. He is convinced of their reliability, and if the circumstances of his life seem to be at odds with what God has said, the fault is not with God's Word but with the psalmist's understanding of how God's Word relates to his circumstance.

Now we get to the crux of the matter. The psalmist confesses that when life was good for him, he went astray. This verb is found four times in the Old Testament, and two of them refer to sinning inadvertently. When life is going well, it is easy to drift and become complacent in our walk with the Lord. The Lord allows us to be afflicted in some way to bring us back, to keep us on the alert. The psalmist indicates the affliction, whatever it was, caused him to get back on the right path and follow God's Word. When we see our problems in this way, we begin to see God's goodness. He is looking out for us and wants to bless us, but He will not if we are going astray.

Verse 68 sums up the first portion of this stanza. The conclusion is *"[The Lord] is good and does good."* No matter what happens, the immutable God is good and will do only that which is good in our lives. The appropriate plea is for God to teach us God's statutes, which are the firm, sure, and permanent words of God. A greater understanding of God's Word will help us discern that God is good and does only what is good on our behalf.

We experience the depth of God's goodness (verses 69–72)

The psalmist's affliction of verse 67 seems to be explained in verse 69. Arrogant, or proud, men are lying about him. My translation goes like this, *"the arrogant have besmeared me with a lie."* The Word is picturesque as it means to plaster over or smear. The Hagia Sofia in Istanbul, Turkey, is one of the most beautiful churches from ancient times. The walls are decorated with beautiful mosaic tiles of gold and precious stones. When the Muslims took over, they plastered over the mosaic murals as their religion forbids anything that might smack of idolatry. In recent years they have been removing the plaster to restore the murals to their original splendour. Here, a godly man is being smeared with a lie to cover up his true character and create an inaccurate and unsightly picture of who he really is. His enemies were guilty of character assassination. This not only ruins our reputation, but it also wounds our pride. It really hurts. We would not be surprised if the psalmist became defensive or struck back with defamatory remarks against his attackers. Instead, however, he determines to be more obedient to God's orders. He will fix his heart on keeping God's Word rather than letting his heart direct his energy on retaliation or self-pity. Affliction from the arrogant has taught him obedience. Learning obedience is an expression of God's goodness. No matter how we try to recover our reputation, we will never be successful. When we commit ourselves to keeping God's Word, He restores the beauty of our character beyond our expectations.

The arrogant are further described as having hearts covered with fat. They are not only unfeeling or insensitive to the pain they are causing, but they are also insensitive to God's Word. In contrast, the psalmist delights in God's law. The word "delight" could mean to caress. A caress is a loving touch that is enjoyable to the one being caressed. We might render this phrase, "I love the feel of your law." God reaches out and touches the psalmist as he meditates on the law of God. Unlike the arrogant, he is not insensitive to God's touch through the Word. He experiences the goodness of God through the Word, and it feels good, especially in a time of affliction at the hands of arrogant men.

The psalmist sums up the experience by saying it was good for him to be afflicted. The good was not for pleasure but for how it profited him spiritually. It was good because he would learn God's statutes. It is a deliberate choice of words as it contrasts the temporal nature of the affliction with the eternal Word of God.

The psalmist learns a great lesson concerning the goodness of God. He has discovered the law from the mouth of God is far more valuable than all the riches he could accumulate. God demonstrates His goodness by giving us His Word, and then He demonstrates it again by doing all that is necessary for us to learn the value of keeping His Word. That may include adversity of some sort. Hebrews 12:5–11 reminds us that God disciplines us as a father disciplines his son. The discipline is for our good, and verse 11 says, *"All discipline for the moment seems not to be joyful, but sorrowful; yet to those who have been trained by it, afterwards it yields the **peaceful** fruit of righteousness."* (emphasis added)

God is good, and He desires to give us the abundant life that is found initially through faith in the Lord Jesus and then maintained through a close walk of fellowship with Him by observing the Word of God. Truly, God is good and lavishes His goodness on us.

Psalm 119:73–80 — Yodh

The Strength of the Afflicted

ı

Yodh.

73 Your hands made me and fashioned me;
    Give me understanding, that I may learn Your
        commandments.
74 May those who fear You see me and be glad,
    Because I wait for Your word.
75 I know, O LORD, that Your judgments are righteous,
    And that in faithfulness You have afflicted me.

76 O may Your lovingkindness comfort me,
    According to Your word to Your servant.
77 May Your compassion come to me that I may live,
    For Your law is my delight.

78 May the arrogant be ashamed, for they subvert me with
        a lie;
    But I shall meditate on Your precepts.
79 May those who fear You turn to me,
    Even those who know Your testimonies.

80 May my heart be blameless in Your statutes,
    So that I will not be ashamed.[10]

---

[10] *New American Standard Bible: 1995 update* 1995 (Psalm 119:73–80). La Habra, CA: The Lockman Foundation.

Henry Wadsworth Longfellow wrote in his poem "Rainy Day":

Into each life some rain must fall
Some days must be dark and dreary.

Every life has had its share of difficulties. Difficulties are part of life. The analogy that Longfellow makes is interesting in that, though rain is a metaphor for hardships, it is also necessary for life. That which is disagreeable is also that which is necessary for growth. Instead of getting upset with the "rain" in our lives, we use adversity to demonstrate our spiritual strength or maturity. It is the children who chant, "rain, rain go away; come again some other day." Mature adults will find it a necessary nuisance at worst and a blessing at best. How do we demonstrate our spiritual strength and maturity?

We demonstrate a godly attitude (verses 73–75)

It helps to know that God made us. Because He made us, He knows us inside and out. Psalm 139:13–16 says, *"For You formed my inward parts; You wove me in my mother's womb. I will give thanks to You, for I am fearfully and wonderfully made; wonderful are your works, and my soul knows it right well. My frame was not hidden from You, when I was made in secret, and skilfully wrought in the depths of the earth; Your eyes have seen my unformed substance; and in Your book were all written the days that were ordained for me, when as yet there was not one of them."* Similarly, Psalm 103:13–14 declares, *"Just as a father has compassion on his children, so the Lord has compassion on those who fear Him. For He Himself knows our frame; He is mindful that we are but dust."*

Since God made us and knows everything about us, He knows how much we can endure.

I Corinthians 10:13 says, *"No temptation (testing) has overtaken you but such as is common to man; and God is faithful, who will not allow you to be tempted beyond what you are able, but with the temptation will provide the way of escape also, so that you will be able to endure it."* How comforting that God knows the limits of our endurance. As a father, I sometimes pushed my sons too hard, and at other times I was too soft on them. Even though I know them quite well, I can never know them as thoroughly as God knows each of us.

God knows us so well He knows how to make us understand His Word and how His commands relate to our lives. Therefore, the psalmist asks God to give him understanding so that he may learn God's commandments with a view of keeping them. The Bible is a reliable communication from God concerning Himself, sin, judgment, salvation, and eternal life. The Bible teaches us how to have fellowship with God, how to have the abundant life Jesus provides, and how God comforts us in the struggles of life.

Having learned God's commandments, we hope (wait) for God's promises to be fulfilled in our lives. Our hope is so tangible that it becomes a testimony and an encouragement for other God-fearing people. We persevere in our faith because of God's promises, and that helps others persevere. We cannot live our lives in isolation. True faith in God will be evident to others. Our hope in God's promises stems from a confidence that God's judgments are always right so that when He afflicts us out of His faithfulness to us, His intention is not to destroy us or to defeat us. His desire is that we will come forth as pure gold from the trials that come our way. He knows just how much we need depending on our level of spiritual development. God's desire is to transform us little by little into the likeness of Christ, which will redound to His glory (Hebrews 12:9–11).

We demonstrate a dependence on God (verses 76–77)
Even though God sends the affliction, we can cry out for God's comfort. Notice the psalmist is not praying for the removal of the affliction but for God's comfort in the midst of the affliction. In this cry for comfort, his appeal is based on God's lovingkindness and

promise to him. We think of the way David was pursued by king Saul prior to becoming king. Saul wanted to kill him, but God had promised David that he would be king. God's promise would encourage him, and though the threat caused David to be on the run in the wilderness, God's lovingkindness kept him safe. There was a time when David lost all hope and took matters into his own hands. It ended badly for him, but David encouraged himself in the Lord. He got back on track when he depended on God's promise to him that he would someday be king.

We can also cry out for God's compassion when life is at its bleakest. Whatever was afflicting the psalmist, he was despondent, and everything looked hopeless. It drained him of all vigour, so he depends on God's compassion to restore the vitality of his life. He prays this because he truly delights in God's covenantal law. This is not a false claim or an empty boast. Neither is it a claim to purity. God can see his heart and knows that what he says is true. There would be times when this was not true, but the prevailing attitude in his life had been that he delighted in God's law. There should be evidence of this.

We demonstrate wisdom in seeking counsel (verses 78–79)

Now we can see what the psalmist was experiencing that caused him to turn to God for comfort and compassion. Arrogant (proud) men were giving false reports about him. Arrogance or pride is incompatible with godliness. These men were like their father, the devil, who slanders God's people. He prays that God would put them to shame. Secular wisdom that leaves God out of the equation proclaims boldly that Christians are wrong in their understanding of origins, women's rights over their bodies, the acceptability of same-sex marriage, and the list goes on. Thank the Lord there are scholars who can answer these charges, but the rest of us would do well to follow the example of the psalmist, *"But I shall meditate on Your precepts."* God's Word should be our primary source for truth.

A secondary source for truth is counsel from those who fear the Lord, those who know God's testimonies. We may derive much encouragement from them. When the psalmist says, *"May those who fear You turn to me,"* he is seeking comfort from godly people, God fearing and God knowing. These are the ones who are devoted to God and are well versed in the Word of God. The two go together. To have knowledge without the fear of God leads to presumption, and to have the fear of God without knowledge leads to superstition. If God's Word is our primary source of truth, godly people are the secondary source of truth. As Christians we need guidance, but we need to be careful of its source. We can now go back to verse 76 and understand that God comforts us primarily through His Word, but God uses godly people as another source of comfort.

We demonstrate a spiritual resolve (verse 80)
This closing prayer indicates the resolve of the psalmist. He prays for a blameless heart as measured against God's statutes, which are fixed and permanent. In keeping with the context of this section of verses, he might be praying that his affliction would not be a means for sin to take root in his life. It would be a time when his defences would be down. It is a spiritual battle, and he is depending on the Lord to keep him true to God's Word. He knows if he were to fail, it would be shameful. He has a desire to lead a shameless life. He has taken his stand for God, and if he were to sin because of the affliction, it would be shameful before men. More importantly, he would be ashamed before God.

God allows affliction in our lives, and Satan would like to bring about our spiritual defeat and shame. Satan sometimes uses his people, the arrogant ones. God, however, provides comfort, abundant life, and counsel through the Word and Christian counsellors. Oh, that we might have a prayerful resolve to be obedient and firm in our convictions (cf. I John 2:28; 3:21; 4:17).

Psalm 119:81–88 — Kaph

Getting a Grip on Reality

ר

Kaph.

81   My soul languishes for Your salvation;
        I wait for Your word.
82   My eyes fail *with longing* for Your word,
        While I say, "When will You comfort me?"
83   Though I have become like a wineskin in the smoke,
        I do not forget Your statutes.

84   How many are the days of Your servant?
        When will You execute judgment on those who
           persecute me?
85   The arrogant have dug pits for me,
        Men who are not in accord with Your law.
86   All Your commandments are faithful;
        They have persecuted me with a lie; help me!
87   They almost destroyed me on earth,
        But as for me, I did not forsake Your precepts.

88   Revive me according to Your lovingkindness,
        So that I may keep the testimony of Your mouth.[11]

---

[11] *New American Standard Bible: 1995 update*. 1995 (Psalm 119:81–88). La Habra, CA: The Lockman Foundation.

Explaining the presence of evil has confounded philosophers throughout history. It is especially confusing when one does not believe in an absolute standard of right and wrong. The biblical worldview sees God as the standard of holiness and anyone acting contrary to His character or activity is sinful. Most people believe in a god or gods but do not see them as a moral standard for right and wrong. Those who do not believe in a supernatural being find it difficult to explain the presence of evil or even to define what is good or bad.

Eastern religions, like Hinduism and Buddhism, have a mystical approach to the problem of evil. They say life is an illusion; nothing is real. We must rid ourselves of the illusion and realize our oneness with the ultimate reality of the oversoul or all-pervading spirit. However, to those who are suffering, it is a small consolation as their pain still hurts.

Westerners tend to be more materialistic as they are influenced by Darwinism and science. They say this material universe is all there is and there is no god. Evil is not a reality, and one cannot say something is good or bad. We cannot put a moral evaluation on anything. Even within the postmodern culture of the times, evil is not a reality because it is up to the individual to discern for himself what is good and what is bad. What is true for one person may not be true for another. That leads to anarchy unless we can determine by majority opinion what should be deemed good or bad. The standard to decide becomes public opinion, and public opinion is very fluid. When talking about same-sex marriage, a recent president said he was evolving in his thinking. He had thought it was wrong, but as pressure from the proponents of same-sex marriage increased, his thinking about the subject evolved to where he thought it was acceptable and possibly even good.

For Christians, who believe in a personal creator God, evil does exist. If God is good and does good (verse 68), then everything contrary to that standard is evil or bad. Part of that evil are the afflictions we experience. It does not help to say they are just an illusion or to redefine it as simply an experience we cannot label as good or bad. It still hurts! It is very real to the person experiencing it.

This stanza of Psalm 119 shows how the Word of God provides the bridge between our afflictions and the reality that is God.

The description of his condition (verses 81–83)
His inner man, the soul, languishes or wastes away. This seems to refer to his emotions. The psalmist yearns for God's salvation or deliverance from his affliction. Whatever he was going through, he was longing for God's deliverance so intensely that his emotional strength was diminished. His longing for God's salvation was not based on a philosophical denial of his problem but on the Word of God. He waits or hopes in God's Word because it is in God's Word that he has the assured expectation that God hears the prayers of the righteous. He demonstrates an intense desire for God's deliverance.

Since his hope is in God's Word, he searches diligently for God's promises found in the Bible. His study of the Word of God is so intense that his eyes are failing or getting tired. His search for the answers to his difficulty is in the primary source of knowledge, God's Word. He demonstrates an intense desire for the promises of God, and he engages his intellect in studying God's Word for answers and assurance.

Physically, he describes his condition as being like a wineskin in the smoke. The wineskin was made of a piece of treated goat hide folded over and stitched together, and the seam was sealed to prevent leakage. The narrow opening would be sealed with a wooden cork.

Treated hide would be soft and supple, but as it got older, in dry weather it would dry out and crack. Wineskins were hung on the main post of a tent where the family would live. The smoke from the cooking fires would waft around the wineskin, which would increase the aging process. A wineskin in the smoke would be dry, brittle, and discoloured. The psalmist is so worn down by his affliction that he feels like a wineskin hanging in the smoke. Even so, no matter how poorly he feels physically, he does not forget God's statutes. He demonstrates an intense perseverance in obedience.

There are two important lessons we have touched on in our study thus far: 1) to forget does not mean that God's statutes would be erased from the psalmist's memory, but that he would, by not forgetting them, continue to act upon them no matter how bad he feels, and 2) there is the deliberate contrast with his deteriorating physical condition and the Word of God that is permanent, enduring, and etched in stone.

When we come to the point we think we cannot endure any longer, we are not to give up. Our hope is in God's promises, and we strengthen our resolve to obey God's statutes. Ephesians 6:10–12 reminds us it is a spiritual battle, one of Satan's fiery darts that God allows in our lives to transform us into His likeness.

The description of his afflictions (verses 84–87)
Verse 84 is one of those rare verses that does not have a synonym for God's Word. We discover two questions that remain unanswered and that he has enemies who are persecuting him unjustly. Difficult times tend to breed doubts and despair. When he asks, *"How many are the days of Your servant?"* the implication is that if God does not do something soon, the psalmist will be long gone! When will God punish the persecutors? If God does not do it soon, the psalmist's enemies will succeed in destroying him. No answer is given; what a feeling of hopelessness.

His enemies have tried to trap him. A common means to trap a wild animal was to dig a deep hole in the ground and cover it with twigs and thatch. These persecutors were trying to set a trap for him. Was it to kill him or just to discredit him? Nehemiah experienced a similar situation in Nehemiah 6:10–13, *"When I entered the house of Shemaiah the son of Delaiah, son of Mehetabel, who was confined at home, he said, 'Let us meet together in the house of God, within the temple, and let us close the doors of the temple, for they are coming to kill you at night.' But I said, 'Should a man like me flee? And could one such as I go into the temple to save his life? I will not go in.' Then I perceived that surely God had not sent him, but he uttered his prophecy against me because Tobiah and Sanballat had hired him. He was hired for this reason, that I might become frightened and act accordingly and sin, so that they might have an evil report in order to reproach me."*

These men are described as arrogant. They are those who do not walk according to God's law. To disregard God's covenantal law is to be arrogant. Most people would not like to be called arrogant or proud, but that is what they are if they do not heed God's Word.

These men tried to trap the psalmist by lying about him. A lie is at the foundation of his persecution. If David is the composer of this psalm, we can think back to when King Saul was pursuing him physically and with the lie that David was trying to usurp the throne. When David fled from his son, Absalom, he had spread rumours that David was not attending to the needs of his people (II Samuel 15:3–6). Even Jesus had many false accusers when he stood on trial. The psalmist contrasts the lie of the arrogant with the faithfulness of God's commandments. God's Word is reliable and infallible while the words of men are not to be trusted. So, the psalmist cries out, "Help me!"

His situation is so desperate that he says his enemies have almost destroyed his earthy life. He is saying they are about to exterminate him, rid the earth of him. In all his trials, as severe as they were, he did not abandon God's precepts. Remember, precepts refer to military-like orders from the highest authority. David nearly perished at the hand of Saul; Daniel could have been devoured in the den of lions; Shadrach, Meshach, and Abednego should have burned up in the fiery furnace; and Jesus did die on the cross. These and many others we could mention never forsook God's will for their lives in the face of death!

The description of his deliverance (verse 88)

Again, the psalmist prays that God would revive him according to God's lovingkindness. It may be that he expected to die at the hands of his enemies (verse 87) or just that he was feeling very low (verses 81–83), but he depended on God to deliver him from death or to lift his spirit and give him the zest for life once again. Whatever it was, he acknowledges his prayer was not based on any personal merit but solely based on the grace or lovingkindness of God. Even though we may be faithful, we still do not deserve God's grace.

He has a wonderful motive for asking God to revive his spirit or to save him from death: so he can heed the testimonies (warning signs) that come from the very mouth of God. God saves us so we may continue to be obedient to Him. If, after the threat has passed, and we forget about God's grace like Israel did so often in the book of Judges, we have failed the test. Satan is victorious and we have lost touch with the ultimate reality that is God Himself.

When faced with a great trial, the worst thing we can do is lose our hope and confidence in God. Worse than that, if after the trial we forget that God's grace saved us, we have lost it is then that the victory is lost!

Every person experiences difficult times. It does not help to deny they exist or to philosophize whether they are good, bad, or neutral. They hurt and sometimes they hurt deeply. We do not alleviate the unpleasantness by abandoning God.   He is the ultimate reality, who helps us deal with evil and will always honour His promises to us through His Word. May we all fervently echo the commitment of our psalm writer, *"But as for me, I did not forsake Your precepts."*

Psalm 119:89–96 — Lamedh

The Eternality of the Word

ל

Lamedh.

89   Forever, O LORD,
      Your word is settled in heaven.

90   Your faithfulness *continues* throughout all generations;
      You established the earth, and it stands.

91   They stand this day according to Your [judgments],
      For all things are Your servants.

92   If Your law had not been my delight,
      Then I would have perished in my affliction.

93   I will never forget Your precepts,
      For by them You have revived me.

94   I am Yours, save me;
      For I have sought Your precepts.

95   The wicked wait for me to destroy me;
      I shall diligently consider Your testimonies.

96   I have seen a limit to all perfection;
      Your commandment is exceedingly broad.[12]

---

[12] *New American Standard Bible: 1995 update.* 1995 (Psalm 119:89–96). La Habra, CA: The Lockman Foundation.

Kids have a wonderful way of remembering something we said many years later, especially if it is something we wish we could take back even if we do not remember it. I cannot help feeling sorry for the person being interviewed by a reporter on TV, and the reporter brings up an obscure clip from another decade and asks the one being interviewed if he still stands by what he said back then. Public persons such as politicians or celebrities have to be very careful what they say because, in all likelihood, it is being recorded. Who among us does not wish we could be consistent in everything we have ever said? It is impossible because we do not know how events will unfold over time. Our knowledge on a particular topic may increase over time, so what we may have thought or said previously may have been a result of our ignorance.

God is not limited by a lack of knowledge; He knows everything completely. Neither is He subject to the boundaries of time. When He speaks, it is with full knowledge and it is unalterable. Some of what He has said applies to a particular time and place. It is true and trustworthy in its context, and the passing of time cannot render it untrustworthy. Since the Word of God is rooted in God's eternality, we can have complete confidence in it.

The proposition — God's Word is eternal (verse 89)
God's Word is forever settled in heaven. The Bible describes heaven as God's dwelling place, but we are not to think of it as a locality. It stands for the realm of God outside of time and space. It is a figure of speech we call a metonym. A metonym is a word used as a substitute for something else. When a news reporter talks about Washington passing a bill, he is not talking about George Washington or the state of Washington or Washington DC. He means the federal government of the United States. Heaven is not just God's dwelling place; it refers to all that pertains to God. God is eternal so His Word is eternal. It never changes. We cannot fix a time for its origin as it has always been. It is not confined to creation

or the temporal as it is fixed in eternity. What is established in eternity is carried out in the physically created universe.

With this truth fixed in our hearts, we will have a deep confidence in the reliability of the Word of God. The rest of this portion of the psalm speaks to that end.

The examples (verses 90–91)

First, the psalmist tells us that God is faithful towards people of all periods of time. What God has settled in eternity is faithfully carried out on earth towards mankind. The Word of God is a product of His faithfulness. As long as there are men on earth, God will faithfully carry out what He has established in heaven towards them. For example, Ephesians 1:3–4 says He chose us (Christians) before He created the world and that He predestined us to be His children. Our standing as redeemed children of God was established in eternity past and nothing can ever change it. God is faithful because He is immutable (unchangeable). We must understand that God's Word may be limited to a certain period of time, but since it was established in eternity, it will never fail during that particular period. God will certainly carry out whatever promises are applicable to us.

Many people like to claim Jeremiah 29:11 as God's promise to Christians, *"'For I know the plans I have for you,' declares the Lord, 'plans for welfare and not for calamity to give you a future and a hope.'"* This is a beautiful promise, but it is directed to the people of Israel whom Nebuchadnezzar had taken captive to Babylon. In fact, the captives did not want to hear this message because they did not want to settle down in Babylon, which the earlier verses were commanding them to do. God was telling them if they obeyed God in this, God would bless them, and God would one day let them return to their homeland of Israel. This is not a blanket promise for all believers for all time unless we do some gymnastics in spiritualizing it. There are plenty of other verses that Christians can take to heart, such as Psalm 138:8, I Corinthians 1:8–9, I Thessalonians 5:24, and Philippians 1:6.

God is faithful towards the earth. He established, or created, the earth and it remains. Reading Genesis. We know God created it with His Word. It remains to this day, but that does not mean it will always remain because God has determined, in eternity, that the heavens (universe) and earth will be destroyed by fire (II Peter 3:7). Then God will make a new heaven and a new earth (Revelation 21:1). Until then this earth remains because of God's faithfulness. I am not afraid of an asteroid hitting the earth, a nuclear war that wipes out the total population of the earth, or any other disaster. I'm not booking my ticket for a colony on Mars!

God is faithful towards all creation. Our text is a little ambiguous here as it does not seem to give an antecedent for the word "they" in verse 91. The NIV renders it as "Your laws," but the subject of this paragraph is creation — first people, then the earth, and then the things in the earth. All things stand or remain because this world and all that is in it is sustained by the Word of God's power (Hebrews 1:2–3; Colossians 1:15–17). Romans 8:22 tells us all of creation is suffering from the results of sin in this world, but it will remain until the time that God has determined for it to be destroyed. In verse 89 we see the words "is settled" (stands firm); in verse 90, "established" and "it stands"; and in verse 91, "they stand." We are to understand that as God has determined in eternity, He has carried out in creation, and all will remain until what He has decided in eternity will be the cessation of all things. He is sustaining all things. There is no evolution. The laws of thermodynamics will remain in place until the time God has determined all should end. As of now, "they stand."

The next line tells us why they stand, *"For all things are Your servants."* They are there at God's command, and they will function as He has created them to function to bring Him glory (Psalm 19:1–

6; Romans 1:19–20). If they could change fundamentally, God's Word is not powerful, is not settled, and is not eternal!

The applications (verses 92–95)

In general, the law of God refers to the whole of scripture, but in a special sense it refers to the covenant the Lord made with His people, the Israelites. When a person of higher standing makes a contract with us that includes penalties for noncompliance as well as great benefits, we would be delighted with that contract should we comply with it. God made a covenant (contract) with His people, and in it He promised great blessings if they would only keep their obligations. The person who set his heart on keeping the law would find his delight in it because God would never fail to keep His promises. The psalmist had set his heart on keeping God's law, and it was his delight. Now he was experiencing some affliction that might have ended in physical death, or perhaps he had lost the vitality of life. Delighting in God's law, because he had found God faithful in keeping His covenant, kept him from death or despondency of spirit.

God had revived the psalmist's spirit, so he makes a solemn commitment never to forget God's precepts or orders. His revived spirit is not conditioned on keeping God's precepts, but it is an indication that he continues in an abiding covenant relationship with God and delights in it.

These verses (92–93) have a prophetic element to them. The violation of the covenantal law resulted in death. No one has been able to keep the provisions of the law perfectly. Only Jesus did, and yet He also died on the cross to pay the penalty for all the violations of the law. As a believer in Jesus Christ, I delight in God's Word, which promises eternal life, which is not dependent on my attempts at leading a holy life, but on faith in the finished work of Christ on the cross. I obey His orders, not to gain merit with God, but because I am accepted in the Beloved.

Once we have trusted in Christ, we can claim our standing with God based on His eternal Word. The psalmist cries out, *"I am Yours."* The Old Testament saint was in a covenant relationship with God through faith, and the New Testament saint is in a familial relationship with God through faith (I John 3:1). Once we are assured of our relationship, we can cry out for deliverance. For the psalmist, there were those who would destroy him. Let us leave it unspecific as to what we might face that would cause us to cry out for God's deliverance. The point is we have the right to cry out to God for our needs no matter what we face because we belong to Him as His children. Our obedience to God's precepts or orders demonstrates the proof that we are His. A person who has no regard for the Word of God and lives a life of self-indulgence can have no assurance of being a child of God and has no claim on God. The psalmist says the wicked were seeking to destroy him, but he was committed to diligently consider God's testimonies. Going back to our definition of testimonies, he is navigating the path that God has charted out for him through the Word, and he is aware there are traps, stones to stumble over, or misleading directions. He, therefore, is paying close attention to God's warning signs, reminders, or urgings to stay on the right path and to avoid the pitfalls. He is determined to carefully study God's Word and then to make the proper application to avoid or overcome the dangers and trials along life's pathway.

The conclusion (verse 96)
We are puzzled that perfection has a limit or an end, but the psalmist says he has seen it. That means it is something he could perceive on earth. God is perfect and His Word is perfect, but they are not of this world. Verse 89 says God's Word stands firm in heaven. No, he is talking about what he has experienced on earth. All perfection on earth has its limits or comes to an end. It is not eternal. In contrast, God's commandment is very broad. (The scriptures as a whole are in the scope of the singular word, "commandment.") God's Word is very broad, wide, extensive, and

comprehensive. It means there is no limit; we would say it is infinite. Therefore, it is a solid foundation for faith.

Where do we put our confidence, in the things of this world that is passing away or in an eternal God, who has communicated His truth to us? As Isaiah 40:6–8 says, *"A voice calls out, 'Call out.' Then he answered, 'What shall I call out?' All flesh is grass, and all its loveliness is like the flower of the field. The grass withers, the flower fades, when the breath of the Lord blows upon it; Surely the people are grass. The grass withers, the flower fades, but the word of our God stands forever."*

II Corinthians 4:17–18 says, *"For momentary, light affliction is producing for us an eternal weight of glory far beyond comparison, while we look not at the things which are seen, but at the things which are not seen; for the things which are seen are temporal, but the things which are not seen are eternal."*

Psalm 119:97–104 — Mem

Loving God's Word

מ

Mem.

97   O how I love Your law!
         It is my meditation all the day.

98   Your commandments make me wiser than my enemies,
         For they are ever mine.

99   I have more insight than all my teachers,
         For Your testimonies are my meditation.

100   I understand more than the aged,
         Because I have observed Your precepts.

101   I have restrained my feet from every evil way,
         That I may keep Your word.

102   I have not turned aside from Your [judgments],
         For You Yourself have taught me.

103   How sweet are Your words to my taste!
         Yes, sweeter than honey to my mouth!

104   From Your precepts I get understanding;
         Therefore I hate every false way.[13]

---

[13] *New American Standard Bible: 1995 update.* 1995 (Psalm 119:97–104). La Habra, CA: The Lockman Foundation.

Growth is a sign of health and progress. We keep track of our children's physical growth each year. Our businesses are measured by volume of sales and increase of profits one year over another. This is also true of churches; numerical growth indicates that something good Is happening. Growth of this kind can be measured by raw data.

Other kinds of growth are more subjective and harder to discern. A child may grow physically, but how do we measure emotional and social growth? We may have a variety of tests, but they are somewhat subjective in nature. What about churches? How do we measure spiritual growth? Though it may be subjectively discerned, it is still possible to determine whether an individual or the whole congregation is progressing spiritually. Accordingly, I have relied on a test to determine whether there is perceptible spiritual growth in my congregation.

1. There will be an increasing love for God and His Word. Is there an eagerness to hear the Word of God and learn more of God?
2. There will be an increasing love for God's people. Do we prefer the company of God's people over unbelievers? Is there a desire to be in church with God's people? Is there a willingness to use our God-given gifts for the edification of believers?
3. There will be a decreasing frequency of sin in our lives. Is there a commitment to integrity and truth? Do we see less gossip and coarse talk and more thanksgiving and wholesome talk?
4. There will be an increasing awareness of the awfulness of sin. Do we laugh at lesser misdeeds, or are we grieved by them? One who draws near to a holy God cannot ignore the seriousness of any offense.

It is not my purpose here to flesh these out any further. I would draw your attention to the first of these: there will be an increasing love for God and His Word. It all begins here. God gave us His Word so that we might know Him and His works. Our love for the Word of God will be demonstrated in tangible ways.

The prevailing attitude of love for God's Word (verse 97)

The psalmist cries out, *"O how I love Your law!"* He does not say he reads it. That is commendable. He does not say he listens to it or does what it says. No, these are all good, but love is more than all of these. Reading, listening to, and obeying the Bible may indicate a love for the Bible, but some who claim to do these really do not love it.

Love is an action of commitment and is the highest expression of devotion. The psalmist is committed to the law of God. He can obey it and speak of it only if he knows it. He can know it only if he reads, studies, and listens to it. This is what he implies when he says, *"It is my meditation all the day."* His thoughts are occupied (concerned) with the law of God throughout the day. He is so familiar with God's Word that it governs every action, conversation, and motive, consciously and unconsciously. God's Word, or the principles of His Word, govern one's thoughts and actions in every situation.

We ask ourselves, "What would please the Lord in this situation?" The more we are students of God's Word and committed by love to follow its directions, the easier the answer to that question comes. As we grow older and have spent years meditating on the Word, it becomes second nature to us. However, we must always be on our guard. Solomon was the wisest man on earth, yet his heart was led astray. The Bible tells us he loved many foreign women. He replaced his love for the law of God with another love. His mind was occupied with how he could please them, not with the Word of God.

The results of loving God's Word (verses 98–100)

A real love for God's Word results in much meditation upon it. It becomes part of our lives. That kind of love for the Bible makes us wiser than our enemies. Enemies desire to make us fall, to defeat us. We need to be wiser than the enemy, and absorbing the Word of God will keep us from defeat. When the psalmist says that God's *"commandments are ever with me,"* he is saying they are his constant companions. This does not mean he carries the Bible under his arm wherever he goes but that the Bible is so fixed in his mind and thoughts that he is never without God's Word.

A good example of this is found in the story of the wilderness temptation of Jesus. He had been forty days in the desert without food and water, but when Satan tempted Him, He was able to resist the temptation with appropriate scripture. Satan wanted Him to fail and attacked Him when He was in a weakened condition. Jesus did not have to hunt for the right passage of scripture. It was fixed in His mind and readily available to resist the devil. Satan also used scripture (inappropriately) to tempt Jesus, but Jesus knew the right scriptural response. We are reminded that the psalmist says in verse 11, *"Your word I have treasured in my heart, that I might not sin against You."*

Then we read that loving God's Word gives the psalmist more insight than his teachers. The more one meditates on the Word, the more spiritual understanding he gains. Meditating on the Word throughout one's life makes it possible to surpass our teachers. We can never learn more than our teachers if we limit our instruction to our teacher. The Word of God is the best instructor of godly wisdom, and through meditation and study we ascend above what our teachers can give us. That is why the psalmist says he meditates on God's testimonies.

He goes one level higher, *"I understand more than the aged."* The aged are men of great wisdom gained through a long life. Almost every culture has a respect for the wisdom of our elders. When we were teenagers and thought we had the world figured out, our parents had to remind us they were not born yesterday. Job 12:12 says, *"Wisdom is with aged men, with long life is understanding."* The word "understand" means to behave more perceptively. His activities are governed by a commitment to observe God's precepts. To observe means to guard, keep, or protect as one would a treasure. The treasure is God's precepts, or orders, as in military orders. We are to guard these orders from the most-high God as a treasure in our hearts with a view to obey them explicitly. Then it is possible to behave more perceptively than those who have gained their wisdom from a lifetime of experience.

A summary of these three verses looks like this:
1. More wise than my enemies
   - God's commandments are my companion
2. More insight than my teachers
   - God's testimonies are my meditation
3. More perception than my elders
   - God's orders are my treasure

The demonstration of love for God's Word (verses 101–102)
We demonstrate our love for God's Word in obeying it as our goal. The psalmist says, *"I have restrained my feet from every evil way."* It is our natural inclination to wander off the right path. Both Proverbs and Jesus warn of the way that leads to death or destruction (Proverbs 14:12; Matthew 7:13). It takes a determination of the will to restrain ourselves from going the wrong direction so that we keep, or obey, God's Word. That is how we treasure God's Word.

On the other hand, loving God is our motivation. We treasure God's judgments in our hearts, and He becomes our teacher. God's judgments are always right but sometimes difficult to understand. We must fix our minds on the righteousness of God's actions and never doubt Him. Then He is able to guide us in the correct understanding of them. If we begin with the premise that God is unjust, we will be closing our hearts to the instruction of God through His Spirit. The New Testament calls it *"quenching the Spirit"* (I Thessalonians 5:19). In the same way, if we have turned aside from His judgments, we will not be in fellowship with God, which hinders His instruction. Though we may be attracted to the teachers who are adept at helping us understand the subject under review, no one helps us understand better than God by His indwelling Spirit, and we love Him for it.

The rewards of loving God's Word (verses 103–104)

God's Word is pleasant. It is more pleasant than honey. The imagery in the original language is that it slides easily into my palate. The word "honey" refers to any sweet, sticky substance besides bees' honey. It sometimes means date or grape syrup. These were used as sweeteners. God's promises are sweet or pleasant to us even when the message is bitter. We have a couple of illustrations of this in Ezekiel 2:8–3:3 and Revelation 10:8–11. God gave Ezekiel a scroll with God's message of destruction of Jerusalem. He was to eat it, meaning he was to be thoroughly familiar with its contents so he could deliver the message of the scroll to Israel. Ezekiel describes the message of the scroll as *"lamentations, mourning, and woe,"* but because it is God's Word, when he devours it, it is as *"sweet as honey in my mouth."* Similarly, in Revelation 10, the apostle John is handed a scroll containing the judgments of God on the world. When he eats it, he says, *"in my mouth it was as sweet as honey; and when I had eaten it, my stomach was made bitter."* God's promises are sweet, but the dreaded import of the message can be very bitter.

God's Word gives us understanding. This is the same word found in verse 100 and can be rendered, *"From Your precepts (orders) I behave more perceptively."* Obedience to God's orders naturally results in right conduct before God, but, more than that, it means our right conduct makes sense. How often do we question a superior's directives, but when we follow his instructions, we understand the wisdom behind it. The result of understood obedience is that we will hate every false way. The false way, which seemed so good and alluring, is now detested in comparison to God's orders. The psalmist has progressed from restraint (verse 101) to abhorrence of the false and evil way.

This stanza began with a declaration of love for God's law. It concludes with a declaration of hate for every false way. The two go together; there is no middle ground. We cannot be comfortable with sin and say that we love God's Word. To love God's Word is to find it sweet even while convicting. To obey God's Word is to find God's ways are best and results in hating the way that is contrary to God's directions.

Psalm 119:105–112 — Nun

A Creed to Follow

I

Nun.

105 Your word is a lamp to my feet
And a light to my path.
106 I have sworn and I will confirm it,
That I will keep Your righteous [judgments].

107 I am exceedingly afflicted;
Revive me, O Lord, according to Your word.
108 O accept the freewill offerings of my mouth, O Lord,
And teach me Your [judgments].
109 My life is continually in my hand,
Yet I do not forget Your law.
110 The wicked have laid a snare for me,
Yet I have not gone astray from Your precepts.

111 I have inherited Your testimonies forever,
For they are the joy of my heart.
112 I have inclined my heart to perform Your statutes
Forever, *even* to the end.[14]

One of the motifs of this psalm likens our lives to a path on which we are walking. We have seen an abundance of imagery that

---

[14] *New American Standard Bible: 1995 update.* 1995 (Psalm 119:105–112). La Habra, CA: The Lockman Foundation.

relates to this theme. Our life's pathway is fraught with obstacles that would cause us either to stumble or go astray, but adherence to God's Word will keep us on track. We find it difficult to adhere to God's Word when we have a casual attitude towards it. When we are not persistent in a daily devotional time, when we treat the services of the church, where the Bible is carefully taught, with indifference, and when we read the Bible without engaging the mind to try to understand it, we demonstrate a lack of real devotion to God and His Word.

One man in our church would come up to the pulpit as soon as the service was over and grab my sermon notes to fill in the gaps that he missed during the delivery of the message. While I was greeting folks after the service, he was pouring over my notes to see what he had missed. One lady was so caught up in a verse-by-verse exposition that she would make sure she did not miss a service. She did not want any gaps in the exposition of the biblical book we happened to be studying at the time. People like these demonstrate a keen devotion to God's Word. When we are devoted to God's Word, we will experience guidance for our lives. The verses in this stanza of Psalm 119 develop this truth.

A promise to keep (verses 105–106)
One of the earliest verses we memorize as children is verse 105. The psalmist affirms an important truth, that God's Word sheds light on life's pathway. We have noted before that there is a path to follow and that it is marked out in God's Word. We have also learned that a path exists because it has been frequented. Others have travelled it before us, so it is not obscure and, if others could follow it, so can we. Most importantly, we have observed that God in His incarnation also walked on that path!

However, there are times when the darkness of night obscures our path. Psalm 23 speaks of the *"valley of the shadow of death,"* which is not to be taken to refer to the time of our death, but to any time of darkness when death or danger lurks. This verse acknowledges that in times of great distress God's Word sheds light on the path ahead. The lamps used in those days cast the light just far enough to take one step at a time. There were no high beams. There is a path God wants us to follow, but there are times we cannot see very far down the road. God's Word is a lamp that gives us enough light for our feet to take one step at a time.

How does one get on that pathway and stay on it? This is when a casual approach to God's Word will not suffice. The psalmist makes a promise with a solemn oath, probably by invoking God as his witness, that he will keep God's righteous judgments. Not only has he made an oath, but he also declares that he will confirm it or that he is determined to keep this oath — he will make it come true. The Bible will be his guide in the dark days of his life. He swears it, he is determined to fulfil his oath, and he will follow what God's Word reveals. That is why it is a lamp and light.

Without that single-minded determination to follow the light of God's Word we will be in danger of falling into sin or straying off the path God wants us to follow. A well-worn Bible is a reliable indication that the owner is on the right path.

Obstacles to overcome (verses 107–110)
The psalmist has made an oath that he would persevere in keeping God's Word, and with these verses we understand some of the obstacles we may encounter on life's pathway. Obstacles are there to divert us from the path and to cause us to lose our commitment and confidence in God's Word.

The first obstacle we encounter is described as affliction. The psalmist does not tell us what the affliction is, but it is a great affliction. An expanded translation would say, *"afflicted to an overwhelming degree."* Apparently, it had either robbed him of all vitality of life, or he genuinely thought death was near.

His response to this great affliction is threefold. First, he prays that God would revive his spirit or to preserve his life. As we have noted many times in this psalm, he prays that God would act according to God's Word. It is an attitude of humility, depending on God's ways and not in his own devices. Also, it is a submissive attitude as he accepts God's will for his life.

His second response to affliction is praise. The freewill offering of his mouth is another way of saying he is praising God even when going through a dark episode in his life. If we are able to sincerely praise God in the dark days, it demonstrates a settled conviction that God's ways are best and that *"God causes all things to work together for good to those who love God, to those who are called according to His purpose"* (Romans 8:28). Then, lastly, he prays that God would teach him God's judgments. He is asking that he would know and understand how God's deliverance is according to the Word. He is asking for more understanding that would deepen his praise. God delights to instruct us in His Word as that deepens our understanding of God and His ways, which results in praise and worship of the deepest sort.

Danger is a second obstacle. *"My life is continually in my hand"* is an expression that one is putting his life in danger. That is, by choosing a course of action he is taking a risk (Judges 12:3; I Samuel 19:5, 28:27). It is to say, "My grasp is not very strong on my life." To say that our lives are in God's hand is to repose trust in God's keeping and care, but the psalmist feels he is in a precarious situation and the danger he senses has weakened his confidence in God. However, he affirms that he has not forgotten God's law. That is, he has not failed to act upon God's Word, and in doing so he could be putting his life in danger.

A final danger is from the wicked who would try to trap him. A trap or a snare has an element of deception. Satan and those who serve him are crafty and clever. Their purpose is to cause Christians to sin and bring disgrace to the cause of Christ. The psalmist declares he has not gone astray from God's precepts. He has carried out God's orders fully. Satan has not trapped him or diverted him from the path God has marked out for him.

When we are fixed on keeping God's Word, it will light up our God-given pathway so that we will not stray from God's directions. Afflictions, danger, and deception will pose no threat to the person who sets his heart and mind on keeping God's righteous judgments.

A future to claim (verses 111–112)
He accepted God's testimonies (reminders, warning signs) as his inheritance. The imagery goes back to the days of Joshua dividing the promised land to the twelve tribes of Israel. Each accepted its allotment with joy. There were two tribes that were not fully satisfied, Ephraim and Manasseh (cf. Joshua 17:14–18). The psalmist shows no dissatisfaction when he receives the testimonies of the Lord as his inheritance. After careful consideration he is able to decern that which really gives him joy (cf. Hebrews 11:13–16, 24–26; 12:2).

In accepting God's testimonies as his inheritance, he inclines, or turns his heart, to carry out God's statutes. The force of his intention is strengthened when he says he will do so until the end of his life. The statutes of God indicate the permanence of God's Word, and the psalmist declares he will carry them out for the length of his life. The scriptures have several stories of individuals who did not follow through for the duration of their lives: Solomon; Rehoboam; Asa; and in the New Testament, Demas.

I am sure we all know of those who did not remain true to the Lord throughout their lives. Somewhere they went back on their oath, and the light of God's Word became so dim they could no longer find the path God wanted them to walk.

Psalm 119:113–120 — Samech

The Battle is the Lord's

O

Samekh.

113	I hate those who are double-minded, But I love Your law.
114	You are my hiding place and my shield; I wait for Your word.
115	Depart from me, evildoers, That I may observe the commandments of my God.
116	Sustain me according to Your word, that I may live; And do not let me be ashamed of my hope.
117	Uphold me that I may be safe, That I may have regard for Your statutes continually.
118	You have rejected all those who wander from Your statutes, For their deceitfulness is useless.
119	You have removed all the wicked of the earth *like* dross; Therefore I love Your testimonies.
120	My flesh trembles for fear of You, And I am afraid of Your judgments.[15]

---

[15] *New American Standard Bible: 1995 update*. 1995 (Psalm 119:113–120). La Habra, CA: The Lockman Foundation.

As noted in the previous portion of this psalm, one of the motifs is that of following the path laid out for us in God's Word. This present stanza presents life as a spiritual battle. Ephesians 6:10–18 is a familiar passage dealing with our spiritual warfare. Many familiar hymns and choruses such as, *"Onward Christian Soldiers,"* and the children's song, *"I'm in the Lord's Army,"* dwell on our spiritual warfare.

In warfare we are confronted with danger, hardships, enemies, and deception. The soldier must depend on the wisdom and experience of his superior officers, his weapons, and his equipment. The same is true in our spiritual battle. We depend on God's infinite wisdom to keep us safe and deploy the right tactics to ensure victory. We depend on our weapons of prayer and the sword of the Spirit, the Word of God. We trust our equipment: the belt of truth; the breastplate of righteousness; the helmet of salvation; and the shoes of the preparation of the gospel of peace, which keep us from slipping back.

Just as a well-trained soldier of today depends on his comrades, we are to depend on one another and help one another. The Christian soldier must never underestimate God's final victory over and judgment of the enemies of the cross. As this stanza concludes in verse 120, we are terrified at what God does to His enemies, which provides a compelling motivation for us to stay on the right side of the battle. In our daily struggles we dare not take God for granted.

The battle (verses 113–115)
We are in a battle, and our foe is described as double-minded. They are duplicitous inwardly and outwardly. The intention is to be deceptive. James 1:8 reminds us that a double-minded person lacks faith and does not receive God's favour. One who has no faith is an enemy of God and, therefore, is our enemy, as well. That is why the psalmist says he hates them, but in contrast to his hatred of the double-minded person is his love for God's law.

In keeping with the poetic parallelism of the verse, the psalmist contrasts the double-minded person with the law of God. The law is consistent, no contradictions. Unlike the law, the enemy is completely untrustworthy. Our Commanding Officer and His law are absolutely reliable when we face the battles of life.

In our conflict, we discover that God is our defence. The psalmist describes Him as a hiding place. It is a place of security and refuge. While King David was fleeing King Saul, he would often hide in the rocky wadis of the Judean wilderness. Here, the psalmist finds God to be his place of security. God is also his shield. We cannot always avoid the battle, so as we step out into the fray, God is our shield or defence. The only way we may experience God and His fulness is to wait for (or hope in) His Word. His hope is in the revealed Word of God. If one is not treasuring God's Word in his heart (Psalm 119:11), he is ignorant of God's character and activities and will be unable to appreciate the refuge and defence found in God Himself.

Now the psalmist tells us the double-minded are evildoers. They are not just those who lack faith but are actively engaged in evil activities. The most nefarious activity they might engage in is to prevent the Christian from observing the commandments of God. The psalmist displays his mindset by shouting out to his enemies to leave him alone because he does not want anything to hinder him from obeying God. We cannot accommodate double-minded evildoers in our lives. We must consider them enemies of our obedience to God. James 4:4 tells us that to be friends with the world is to be hostile towards God. That does not even offer a fence to sit on. There is no middle ground.

The resource (verses 116–117)
In our spiritual battle we have a wonderful resource, prayer. This echoes the passage in Ephesians 6 when describing the Christian's armour. It concludes with verse 18, *"With all prayer and petition*

pray at all times in the Spirit." In verses 116–117 we have two prayers: 1) *"Sustain me"* and 2) *"Uphold me."*

When the psalmist prays for God to sustain him, he is requesting physical support. We might say he is asking God to lend him a hand. His confidence in praying in this manner is because God had promised His strength to all who rely on Him. He has shown his reliance on God by devoting himself to the assimilation of God's Word in his life and by disassociating himself from the evildoers. The result of God giving him physical strength is that he would live, or be revived physically, and that he would not be ashamed for having put his hope in God. According to the *Theological Workbook of the Old Testament*, the word for "hope" here is a noun found only two times in the Old Testament (Psalm 119:116; 146:5), and "it refers to God and His Word as the hope of the psalmist."[16]

Then his prayer that God would uphold him is a prayer for inner or spiritual strength. His desire to be safe indicates a concern that he would succumb to the temptations that his enemies use to lure him away from God. This is reinforced by the second line in which the psalmist desires never to fail to regard God's statutes. God's statutes are permanent, and he longs to permanently regard them. The enemy devises schemes to lure him away from the safety and security of God and His Word. In both these requests he shows he is entirely dependent on God for spiritual victory.

The victory (verses 118–119)
Now we see God's reaction to the enemy. The word "rejected" means that God has made light of His enemies or that He considers them worthless. They are like dust on our bathroom scale. We do not carefully wipe off every bit of dust that may be there before we

---

[16] Cohen, G. G. (1999). 2232 שָׂבַר. In R. L. Harris, G. L. Archer Jr., & B. K. Waltke (Eds.), *Theological Wordbook of the Old Testament* (electronic ed., p. 870). Moody Press.

weigh ourselves. That dust is inconsequential. We disregard it as having any significance in registering our weight. Anyone who wanders or strays from keeping God's statutes are treated as the dust on the scale, worthless, because their deceitfulness, or treachery, is useless, or a lie. All the deceptions of the enemy to lure us into abandoning God are a lie, falsehood. God is a God of all truth, and in Him there is no lie, so when He confronts those who are deceitful, He treats them as of no consequence. Notice that God's rejection of them is in the past tense. It has not happened yet as God is patiently waiting for them to repent as in II Peter 3:9. If they never repent in this the day of salvation, they will be rejected by God. It is rendered in the past tense because it is so certain it is as if it has already taken place. The enemy is defeated, and a defeated enemy is of no consequence.

It gets even more dramatic in verse 119. Not only is the enemy defeated, but the enemy is also judged. A literal rendering of this verse might be, *"Dross! You have put an end to all the wicked of the earth!"* God has put the wicked into the furnace of His judgment, and the wicked are like the impurities of dross that are thrown out. Again, it is in the past tense because it is as good as done!

The response of the psalmist is classic, *"Therefore I love Your testimonies."* God's Word, which serves as reminders or warning signs along life's pathway, keeps us from being considered wicked by God and therefore kept from being judged as inconsequential or as dross.

The reaction (verse 120)
When contemplating God's judgment on the wicked, the psalmist's reaction is of horror. His flesh trembles or shudders in fear of God. This is more than a mild case of goose bumps, and it is much more than just revering God. The word "fear" means to dread and is often found in context with trembling or quaking. He does not shout with glee at the demise of the wicked. He is afraid of God's

judgments because there is no one who is perfectly right with God. How can any of us stand before God the righteous judge? It would be very foolish for anyone to take God lightly. Unfortunately, many treat God as inconsequential and of no use.

> Hebrews 10:31, *"It is a terrifying thing to fall into the hands of the living God."*
> Hebrews 12:29, *"For our God is a consuming fire."*
> Hebrews 9:27, *"...it is appointed for men to die once and after this comes judgment...."*
> But then we are reassured by Romans 8:1, *"Therefore there is now no condemnation for those who are in Christ Jesus."*

For those of us who have trusted in the finished work of Christ on the cross in paying the penalty for our sins, we have nothing to fear, but we do not take God for granted. As we have observed in this psalm, the psalmist's pursuit of God through his commitment to God's Word is the affirmation that he is on the path pleasing to God.

To the one who is not submitting to God and His Word, I offer this final plea from the Bible,
II Corinthians 6:2b, *"Behold, now is 'the acceptable time,' behold, now is the day of salvation."* This lifetime is the time to become a child of God through faith in Jesus. After we pass on, there is no more opportunity for salvation.

Psalm 119:121–128 — Ayin

When God Acts

ע

Ayin.

121   I have done justice and righteousness;
Do not leave me to my oppressors.

122   Be surety for Your servant for good;
Do not let the arrogant oppress me.

123   My eyes fail *with longing* for Your salvation
And for Your righteous word.

124   Deal with Your servant according to Your lovingkindness
And teach me Your statutes.

125   I am Your servant; give me understanding,
That I may know Your testimonies.

126   It is time for the LORD to act,
For they have broken Your law.

127   Therefore I love Your commandments
Above gold, yes, above fine gold.

128   Therefore I esteem right all *Your* precepts concerning
everything,
I hate every false way.[17]

---

[17] *New American Standard Bible: 1995 update.* 1995 (Psalm 119:121–128). La Habra, CA: The Lockman Foundation.

Whenever we have a problem, trial, or need, we go to God in prayer asking for His help. We plead for Him to solve the problem or to make us strong in the trial. We are invited to come to God in prayer. Jesus taught His disciples, *"give us this day our daily bread...and do not lead us into temptation, but deliver us from evil"* (Matthew 6:11, 13). James 4:2 says, *"...you do not have because you do not ask."* James also reminds us in 1:17, *"Every good thing given and every perfect gift is from above, coming down from the Father of lights, with whom there is no variation or shifting shadow."* Looking at the Sermon on the Mount again we read these words in Matthew 7:7–11, *"Ask, and it will be given to you; seek, and you will find; knock, and it will be opened to you. For everyone who asks receives, and he who seeks finds, and to him who knocks it will be opened. Or what man is there among you who, when his son asks for a loaf, will give him a stone? Or if he asks for a fish, he will not give him a snake, will he? If you then being evil, know how to give good gifts to your children, how much more will your Father who is in heaven give what is good to those who ask Him!"* Yes, we are encouraged to bring our burdens to the Lord in prayer.

However, on what basis does God listen to our requests in prayer? We are cautioned in Psalm 66:18, *"If I regard wickedness in my heart, the Lord will not hear me."* We must assume that if we are harbouring sin in our lives, meaning that we are unrepentant about known sin, God is not obligated to respond to our prayers. Actions do have consequences. In this portion of Psalm 119 we see a series of cause and effects — action and reactions.

The words "done," "deal," and "act" found in verses 121, 124, 126, respectively, are all derived from the same root word "to do." These form the basis for the three headings for this portion, and we observe that God acts according to our activities and His Word.

Activities that ensure God's protection (verses 121–123)

The psalmist makes a claim that he has done justice and righteousness. This is a bold claim to make before God as God sees and knows the veracity of the claim. The psalmist's heart does not convict him, and he is confident in this statement. The word "justice" would be better rendered "judgment." If David is the author of the psalm, it stands to reason that as king he would judge the nation of Israel. While passing judgment on the cases before him, he had confidence that he had judged righteously. He made his decisions without bias or prejudice, and he was not coerced by politics or bribes. Asaph, the poet, testifies of King David in Psalm 78:72, *"So he, David, shepherded them according to the integrity of his heart, and guided them with his skilful hands."*

Rulers are notorious for their corruption, and it is a rarity to find a politician known for his honesty and integrity. But this should not be limited to those in a position of authority. A holy God demands that all people act justly without prejudice. We read the words of Micah 6:8, *"He has told you, O man, what is good; and what does the Lord require of you but to do justice, to love kindness, and to walk humbly with your God?"* The Lord Jesus gave us the Golden Rule in Matthew 7:12, *"In everything, therefore, treat people the same way you want them to treat you, for this is the Law and the Prophets."* We are reminded of Habakkuk crying out to the Lord because of the injustice, or violence, the common people were committing in the land. Ironically, he questioned God concerning God's justice in not punishing the people for their cruelty to one another.

When we search our hearts and with a clear conscience declare before God that we have acted justly with our neighbour, then we may be assured of God's attentiveness to our prayers. Here, the psalmist is at the mercy of his oppressors, those who are not treating him justly. He asks God not to abandon him to those who are oppressing him because he has a clear conscience with respect to how he has treated others.

Next, he prays that God would stand surety for him. One way this word is used is to take another's interests as our own. In doing so we take the other person under our protection. If my brother wanted to take a loan from the bank, he could ask me to stand surety for him since my credit rating is good. If he defaulted on the loan, the bank would come after me to make the necessary payments. In the New Testament, Jesus has become our surety or security. The writer to the Hebrews declares, *"so much more also Jesus has become the guarantee (surety) of a better covenant"* (Hebrews 7:22). Paul states in Ephesians 1:13–14 concerning the Holy Spirit, *"...having also believed, you were sealed in Him with the Holy Spirit of promise, who is given as a pledge of our inheritance, with a view to the redemption of God's own possession, to the praise of His glory."* God is our surety and not our actions. We do not trust in our good works to guarantee our eternal redemption. We trust in the finished work of Christ on the cross.

Then the psalmist requests that God would not allow the arrogant or proud to oppress him. An arrogant person is so full of himself that he has no room for God in his life. Such a person seeks ways to take advantage of others for his own benefit. Pride is in direct opposition to godliness. The psalmist feels threatened by these arrogant ones, so he cries out to God for deliverance from their evil schemes.

He confidently prays for deliverance because he, himself, is not guilty of such behaviour. We must not think that God is petty in that He will listen to a prayer only because we have earned the right by our good actions. Our right to the throne of God is through Jesus Christ by His Spirit. However, our wrong activities will exclude us from the privilege we have in prayer. What parent would reward a child for bad behaviour by giving in to his request? The child has a right to ask because of his position in the family, but the parent has the option of refusing the petition of the child if he has persistently disobeyed. It is a matter of justice carried out with love.

The psalmist further demonstrates a godly attitude by declaring that his eyes fail for God's deliverance and for God's righteous promises. He speaks of an intense longing and desire. While others may try to save themselves by bribing their oppressors or other nefarious activities, the psalmist will not resort to that. Instead he will maintain his integrity and trust only in God and God's promises in the Word of God. When King Asa was confronted by a large enemy army, he cried out to God, *"Lord, there is no one besides You to help in the battle between the powerful and those who have no strength; so help, O Lord our God, for we trust in You, and in Your name have come against this multitude. O Lord, You are our God; let not man prevail against You"* (II Chronicles 14:11).

Activity of God that ensures further obedience (verses 124–125)
In these two verses is a prayer for God to act on behalf of the psalmist, who identifies himself as God's servant. This is the second of three times he calls himself a servant of God in this stanza, which indicates his humility in approaching the Lord in prayer for his needs. He does not want God to do any special favours for him, as that would be contrary to God's justice. Instead, he wants God to deal with him in accordance with God's lovingkindness. To be more specific, he requests the Lord to teach him God's statutes. It would be an act of God's lovingkindness to teach him the statutes of God. It could also be a question of how God's lovingkindness is seen in his oppression as determined by the permanent Word of God. For instance, what does God's Word teach us what "good" means in Romans 8:28 when we experience trials of any kind?

Again, he demonstrates his humility in calling himself a servant of God when he asks for understanding so that he may know the Lord's testimonies. As a loyal servant, it is necessary for him to know and understand the will of his Master. So, he requests God to deal with him on the basis of the Lord's lovingkindness and on the basis of his attitude as a servant. He desires the Lord to teach him the enduring Word of God so that he may understand and know God's warning signs and reminders with the goal of always doing justice and righteousness.

Activity of God in judgment of the disobedient (verses 126–128)

It is time for the Lord to act because the oppressors of verses 121–122 have broken God's Law. God's Law is summed up in two great commandments: *"love the Lord your God with all your heart and with all your soul and with all your might"* (Deuteronomy 6:4), and *"love your neighbour as yourself"* (Leviticus 19:18). Leviticus 19 is devoted to instructions on how to treat people fairly and justly. The oppressors of the psalmist were violating the clear commands of God; they were wicked. The time was right for God's judgment on them for they had broken or invalidated God's Law in that they totally ignored it.

On the other hand, the psalmist's reaction to God's Law as summarized in the two great commandments is threefold:

1. I love Your commandments more than great wealth.
2. I esteem right all Your precepts (orders) in totality. It might be rendered, "I keep your orders precisely."
3. I hate every false way (cf. verse 104). In verse 120 of the previous stanza, he trembles and fears the Lord and is afraid of God's judgments. These last few lines are not a contradiction of verse 120 but complimentary.

William Cowper wrote these lines:
"Ye that love the Lord, hate evil."
He that loves a tree hates the worm that consumes it.
He that loves a garment hates the moth that eats it.

He that loveth life abhoreth death;
And he that loves the Lord hates everything that offends Him.
Let men take heed to this, who are in love of their sins:
How can the love of God be in them?

Psalm 119:129–136 — Pe

The Transforming Power of God's Word

פ

Pe.

129   Your testimonies are wonderful;
        Therefore my soul observes them.
130   The unfolding of Your words gives light;
        It gives understanding to the simple.
131   I opened my mouth wide and panted,
        For I longed for Your commandments.

132   Turn to me and be gracious to me,
        After Your manner with those who love Your name.
133   Establish my footsteps in Your word,
        And do not let any iniquity have dominion over me.
134   Redeem me from the oppression of man,
        That I may keep Your precepts.
135   Make Your face shine upon Your servant,
        And teach me Your statutes.

136   My eyes shed streams of water,
        Because they do not keep Your law.[18]

---

[18] *New American Standard Bible: 1995 update* 1995 (Psalm 119:129–136). La Habra, CA: The Lockman Foundation.

According to II Timothy 3:16 Scripture was breathed out by God. And since God is the source of the Bible, it is trustworthy and authoritative. It is described in Hebrews 4:12 as

"living and active and sharper than any two-edged sword." There is
    power in God's Word as
we read and study it. Paul tells us in Romans 1:16 that the gospel
    "is the power of God for
Salvation." Therefore, the Bible is no ordinary book that gives us
    information or instruction
on how to live our lives. It is a communication from God that
    transforms us from within by
His own power.

We are reminded of the power of God's Word in creation. He commanded the light to appear and there was light. During Jesus' ministry on earth He commanded the wind and sea to be calm and all became calm. He ordered the demons to come out and they could not resist His authority. Now we have the written Word of God, and it powerfully works in our lives to transform us into the image of Jesus. The reading, study, and meditation of God's Word transforms our attitudes and thoughts. Romans 12:2 instructs us to *"not be conformed to this world, but be transformed by the renewing of your mind."* We renew our minds and the way we think by being students of the Bible, God's Word.

Transforming my attitude towards the Word of God (verses 129–131)

As we delve into the Scriptures, we discover that God's testimonies are wonderful. As a synonym for God's Word, the word "testimonies" carries the thought of warning signs or reminders. Previously I noted the psalmist delighted in God's testimonies because they remind him of the pitfalls on the path of life. They serve as warning signs for us to be careful in negotiating the road God has charted out for us to follow. Now, the psalmist declares that God's testimonies are wonderful. This emphasizes the intrinsic value of God's Word. It is wonderful, marvelous, or extraordinary just because it is God's Word.

Do we still have an awe at the wonder of God's Word? When we consider that God is the source and how it was recorded and preserved for us in our generation, we should be full of awe. When we see its accuracy in describing nature, history, and how it lays out the story of redemption without any contradictions and inconsistencies, we marvel. The fulfilment of prophecy within its pages is mind-boggling. Yes, God's Word is wonderful.

If we are able to perceive the marvel of God's Word, then we should respond to it in an appropriate manner. The psalmist's response is that he would observe it. The word "observe" means attentive contemplation. He would study it carefully until he could understand it as fully as possible. When we discover that God's Word is intrinsically good and wonderful, we would then endeavor to study and meditate on it with great devotion.

Not only is the Bible intrinsically wonderful, but it is also extrinsically valuable. The psalmist tells us the *"unfolding of Your words gives light."* God's Word will shed light as we study it. This would be the expected result of verse 129. God's Word gives understanding to the simple. In the wisdom literature of the Old Testament there are three classes of people: 1) the wise, 2) the fool, and 3) the simple. The wise person is one who fears the Lord, the fool says there is no God, and the simple is a naïve person who may choose the way of the wise or go the way of the fool. If even a simple person begins to read the Bible, the supernatural power of God's Word will shed light on the true nature of this world and of spiritual realities for him. It is marvelous to see how some people come to Christ by merely reading God's Word. Others may need a little help like the Ethiopian eunuch in Acts 8. However, it was the Scripture that worked in his heart that prepared the way for Philip's witness. The two disciples on the way to Emmaus on resurrection Sunday were confused and dejected when Jesus joined them on their journey and explained from the Scriptures how the events of the last three days were a fulfilment of prophecy. Their own testimony was that while Jesus spoke to them of the scriptures, their hearts were burning within them.

As Jesus begins to talk to them, He says, *"O foolish men and slow of heart."* When Jesus calls them "foolish," He uses a different word than the customary word for a fool who has set his heart against God. This word would be like the word "simple," meaning ignorant. Whenever we read or study the Bible, we must have an attitude of wonder towards it because it is God's Word and an acknowledgment that when it comes to God's Word we are simple or ignorant in our understanding. We do need to be instructed by God through His Word. So, the psalmist's response is that he, like a thirsty animal panting for water, is yearning for God's commandments. Was he admitting that his understanding of God's ways was so limited that he was as a simple or a naïve person? He was anxious to learn and not remain simple or naïve.

Transforming my attitude towards prayer (verses 132–135)

The Bible is the vehicle that leads us to greater communion with God. First, the psalmist prays for God's favor. (Verse 132 is one of the few verses that does not have any of the synonyms for the Bible.) When God turns towards us, it means that He turns towards us with favor. The psalmist also prays that God would be gracious to him. We cannot read God's Word just for the nice things that pertain to us (and there are many). We will also be confronted by the condemnation and consequences of sin. The Holy Spirit uses the Word to convict us of sin, righteousness, and judgment (John 16:8). Our sin and shortcomings compel us to seek God's favor and grace. Incidentally, it is never God who turns from us but we who have turned from Him. *"All of us like sheep have gone astray, each of us has turned to his own way"* (Isaiah 53:6). We are like the lost sheep that is found by the shepherd. God never turned from us, but when the Spirit of God speaks to our hearts through the Word so that we are repentant, we find that as we turn back, He was there all along. When the prodigal son had not reached home, his father was there looking down the road, waiting for him and then ran to meet and embrace him.

This is in keeping with God's compassion towards those who are His. John 1:12 says, *"But as many as received Him, to them He gave the right to become children of God, even to those who believe in His name."* Again, in I John 3:1, *"See how great a love the Father has bestowed on us, that we would be called children of God; and such we are."* We are God's children, and the Bible affirms over and over that God treats His children with love and compassion. The psalmist prays, *"be gracious to me, after Your manner with those who love Your name."* Or that God would treat him as one of His people. That would be as a descendent of Abraham with whom God had made an unconditional covenant. New Testament saints are children of God by a new covenant, and He is our gracious heavenly Father who has favoured us with salvation. God's favour may include unpleasantness in our lives, but that is always for our good (Hebrews 12:5-11; Psalm 119:67, 71, 75). We pray for God's favour and grace because of our failures, sin, and weaknesses. My paraphrase would be, "Treat me as one of Your children."

Next, we pray for victory over temptation, or "Don't let sin be my master." We can pray that God would make our steps along life's journey firm in His Word. It is useless for us to endeavor to keep to the path God has marked out for us by our own wisdom and strength. It requires the power of God to lead a God-pleasing, righteous life. We do not want any iniquity or sin to have power over us. Paul reminds us in Romans 6:14, *"For sin shall not be master over you, for you are not under law but under grace."* The Bible points out the insidious nature of sin, and when we recognize its power to keep us in its grasp, we cry out to the Lord to free us from its bondage. Only God can free us. The writer to the Hebrews tells us to, *"lay aside every encumbrance and the sin which so easily entangles us and let us run with endurance the race that is set before us"* (Hebrews 12:1). Sin has great power to enslave us, and we are not to treat it lightly.

Then we pray for freedom to obey God. Unbelievers are a source of pressure upon the believer to cause him to sin. The word "redeem" means to deliver or to buy back and be freed from one master to serve another master. The psalmist desires to be delivered from the oppression of man. He is not speaking of any specific man but of the laws, culture, customs, and society of man. This may include family obligations and expectations from those who do not acknowledge Jesus as Lord. He desires this deliverance so that he may keep God's precepts. He desires to carefully obey God's orders as they come from the highest of all authority. A person absorbed by the Word of God will pray that all hindrances to the free exercise of his faith would be removed. I've rendered it this way, "Don't let me be under pressure from the world of unbelievers to sin."

Finally, we pray for God's instruction. This is a recurring theme in Psalm 119, but here there is an added element that gives poignancy to the request. The psalmist prays that God's face would shine upon him, God's servant. As God's servant, he is humbly asking for God's favour and approval. God's favour would be to have God teach him the statutes of the Lord. When a master looks with disapproval on a servant, his face would be "dark" or angry. On the other hand, for the master's face to "shine" would be with a smile and approval. Our desire should be to have God approve of us and to instruct us in His Word so that we may know how to keep expecting God's approval and favour.

Transforming my attitude towards sinners (verse 136)

Having a deeper communion with God will instil in us a heart of compassion for those who are outside of God's approval. The psalmist says he weeps uncontrollably because there are those who do not keep, or obey, God's law. He hates every false way (verses 104, 128) but he has compassion for the disobedient. These are those who are ignorant that God's Word is wonderful and that it sheds light on our journey through life. They are walking in darkness and are slaves to sin (II Corinthians 4:4; Romans 6:6, 14–17).

Jesus said, *"Lift up your eyes and look on the fields, that they are white for harvest"* (John 4:35) and *"The harvest is plentiful, but the workers are few. Therefore, beseech the Lord of the harvest to send out workers into His harvest"* (Matthew 9:37–38).

There have been times when taking the train in India and approaching New Delhi that we would be travelling past mile after mile of slums with hundreds of thousands living in squalor and spiritual darkness. I found myself with tears in my eyes as I thought of their bondage to sin and that there were so few willing to reach them with the transformative power of God's Word. These people are missing out on God's approval and favour.

Maybe there are so few willing to join the harvest because Christians have not been awestruck by the wonder of God's Word. Could it be that we are in bondage to a sin and have not experienced God's grace in our own lives? Instead of seeing our culture as being oppressive, we revel in the ways of this world and embrace them.

Oh, may we see ourselves as servants of God who are ignorant and lacking in understanding of God's ways. We need His favour in instructing us in the Word He has so graciously given us so that we might see the world through His eyes. He loved the world of sinful man so much that He gave His own Son to die for us. May we give ourselves to learn of Him and serve Him. May He give us eyes that weep from hearts of compassion for those who do not keep His law because they do not know any better.

Psalm 119:137–144 — Tsadhe

Some Intrinsic Qualities of God's Word

צ

Tsadhe.

137   Righteous are You, O LORD,
       And upright are Your judgments.
138   You have commanded Your testimonies in
       righteousness
       And exceeding faithfulness.
139   My zeal has consumed me,
       Because my adversaries have forgotten Your words.

140   Your word is very pure,
       Therefore Your servant loves it.
141   I am small and despised,
       Yet I do not forget Your precepts.

142   Your righteousness is an everlasting righteousness,
       And Your law is truth.
143   Trouble and anguish have come upon me,
       Yet Your commandments are my delight.
144   Your testimonies are righteous forever;
       Give me understanding that I may live.[19]

---

[19] *New American Standard Bible: 1995 update.* 1995 (Psalm 119:137–144). La Habra, CA: The Lockman Foundation.

The manner in which we approach God's Word determines our response to it. Sadly, there are prominent Christian leaders who are leading God's people away from the authority of the Bible in subtle ways. There are those who claim that only the very words of Jesus constitute the Word of God and we should pay more careful attention to the words in red. Others are declaring the Old Testament has little value for Christians, so we should stick to the New Testament almost exclusively. Then there are those who see it as a magical book and if we find a verse (out of context) that appeals to us, we can claim it as God speaking to us directly. This leads to disillusionment when things do not work out satisfactorily.

The Bible must be approached as divinely inspired, authoritative, and wholly accurate. Anything less will result in an imperfect vision of God, an incomplete understanding of God's work in redemption, and an inept competency in carrying out God's work. The way God's Word is handled these days, it is no wonder that our zeal for spiritual truth and godly living has diminished greatly in recent years.

A trend has taken place where the experience of worship has superseded the object of worship. Worship has devolved into a "feel good" moment rather than approaching God through the revelation of Himself in the Bible to praise Him, pray to Him, and learn of Him. In verse 129 we noted the intrinsic value of God's Word, and now we find the intrinsic quality of God's Word stirs our hearts with zeal. God's Word is reliable, pure, and eternal in its fulness and entirety.

The reliability of God's Word (verses 137–139)
Why is God's Word reliable? The Lord, who is the covenant-keeping God of His people, is the source of Scripture, and He is declared to be righteous. This declaration is very emphatic in its assertion. Righteousness is correct judgments or activities as measured against a normative standard. God has set the standard and

revealed it in His Word, and the psalmist, after carefully considering the activities of God in His dealings with the people of His covenant, declares the Lord is righteous. God measures up to His own standard of righteousness and gains the approval of the psalmist. God is scrutinized and not found wanting. He is righteous.

The verse goes on to say that God's judgments are upright or correct. Whatever God has determined, or judged, is right. So now, the psalmist has judged God by God's own judgments. God is just.

Then the psalmist observes that this righteous and just God has commanded (appointed) His testimonies in (out of) righteousness. He has observed that the testimonies of God emanate from God's righteousness and exceeding faithfulness. The testimonies, or warning signs (reminders), were given out of the highest degree of reliability because, as he has already observed, God is righteous and His judgments are right. Therefore, that which God has commanded or appointed must be righteous and reliable.

The reliability of God's Word causes the psalmist to be zealous, or passionate, for it. This zeal consumes him, or wears him out, because his adversaries have forgotten God's words. His zeal causes him to stand up and defend the Word of God in the face of those who were ignoring it. His zeal burned hotter and hotter as his enemies' zeal grew colder.

As more and more people are turning away from God's Word, we who see its worth ought to be passionately defending it against the cold tide of disbelief. O for a zeal to the point of exhaustion! Let's pray for a zeal that comes from an absorption of God's Word.

The purity of God's Word (verses 140–141)
God's Word is very pure. The word "pure" has the meaning of being refined, and the word "very" means to the highest degree. Proverbs 30:5a says, *"Every word of God is tested."* The testing of

God's Word is through the personal application of it to our lives. We discover that it is 100 percent accurate and a reliable guide for a life pleasing to God.

Therefore, the psalmist, calling himself God's servant, says that he loves it. His declaration of love for the Word of God is a settled conviction and not just a passing emotion. In calling himself a servant, he further describes his humility by saying he is small and despised. He sees himself as insignificant (like a child in the world of adults) and of no consequence. These are proper attitudes of a servant, but they do not absolve him from acting on his Master's orders (precepts). Humility is a good attitude but not an excuse for coldness towards God and His commands. Convinced of the purity of God's orders, the psalmist carries them out with all humility. Our low estate does not exempt us from obedience to God. We cannot leave the work of God for the leaders and prominent Christians.

The eternality of God's Word (verses 142–144)
The foundation for the eternality of God's Word is found in the eternality of God's righteousness. God has given His Word as a righteous act because He Himself is righteous. Therefore, God's law is truth, and truth is eternal. Jesus, in His High Priestly prayer in John 17:17, says, *"Sanctify them in the truth; Your word is truth."* As God in the flesh, He declares in John 14:6 that He is the truth.

The psalmist goes on to say in verse 144 that God's testimonies (warning signs, reminders) are righteous forever. In his experience, in following God's testimonies, he has discovered that God's testimonies are righteous, and he has confidence that they will be righteous forever. This would certainly be correct if God's righteousness is everlasting and His law is true.

His response is that he delights in God's commandments while experiencing trouble and anguish. When he says they have come upon him, they have come upon him, not as a consequence of any conduct on his part, but that they just happen to be there. That is the normal experience of life, but when we have the right approach to the Word of God, we find delight in it and not dwell on our problems. He also responds by requesting the Lord to give him more life-giving insights. God's Word has the power to lift our spirits as we struggle to cope with the pressures of our ordinary lives.

In these last three verses, I do not see that God has removed the psalmist's troubles, nor is there any indication that he has overcome them. They are still present, and, though he experiences the anguish of them, he still delights himself in God's commandments and wants greater insight into what the Lord has revealed in His Word. Could it be that he perceives that the trials are temporal, only for this lifetime, and the Word is eternal? Why focus on something that won't last when we can focus on that which is eternal?

I wonder how zealous I am for the things of the Lord. As I look back over these verses, I find four evidences of zeal: 1) the psalmist <u>loves</u> God's Word (verse 140); 2) he <u>does not forget</u> it – he acts upon it (verse 141); 3) he <u>delights</u> in the Word (verse 143); and 4) he <u>desires to gain more insight</u> into God's Word (verse 144). That is a good yardstick to see how we measure up.

Psalm 119:145–152 — Qoph

How to Pray When in Distress

ק

Qoph.

145	I cried with all my heart; answer me, O LORD! I will observe Your statutes.
146	I cried to You; save me And I shall keep Your testimonies.
147	I rise before dawn and cry for help; I wait for Your words.
148	My eyes anticipate the night watches, That I may meditate on Your word.
149	Hear my voice according to Your lovingkindness; Revive me, O LORD, according to Your [judgments].
150	Those who follow after wickedness draw near; They are far from Your law.
151	You are near, O LORD, And all Your commandments are truth.
152	Of old I have known from Your testimonies That You have founded them forever.[20]

The subject of prayer is inexhaustible. Many questions arise concerning prayer, but even if we do not understand everything

---

[20] *New American Standard Bible: 1995 update*. 1995 (Psalm 119:145–152). La Habra, CA: The Lockman Foundation.

and do not have all our questions answered concerning prayer, we know that it is vital for the life of a Christian. The theology of prayer is probably not as important as the practice of prayer.

Every person experiences distressful periods in his life. It is during these periods that we are driven to our knees in prayer and to acknowledge our dependence on God. The psalmist has described some of the adversity he has faced as one who is fully devoted to God. Now, in this portion of Psalm 119, he cries out to God in his distress. As we learn from his example, effective prayers will be consistent with the Word of God.

Pray earnestly (verses 145–148)
During times of great stress, we come to God in prayer to lay the burdens of our heart before Him. The intensity of our prayers is commensurate with the difficulty at hand. However, intensity alone does not move the heart of God. There must be some conditions that, when in place, we may have confidence that God will turn a sympathetic ear to our prayers. That is not to say that God does not pay attention to us unless every condition is perfectly in place, but that we may have confidence in approaching God. When we need help from someone we have ignored, we have little confidence in coming to him for assistance.

The first condition is that the psalmist cries out with his whole heart. Twice he cries out to the Lord (verses 145–146), and then in verse 147 he uses a much more intense word when he says, *"I...cry for help."* The repetition of the first word and the intensity of the word in verse 147 describes a person who is earnestly calling on God in his time of trouble.

His cry to the Lord is *"with all my heart."* We have noted before that when we approach God, it must be with an undivided heart. Some people cover all bases by praying to various gods, saints, spirits, as well as knocking on wood or carrying a lucky rabbit's foot. If the prayer were to be answered, to whom would we give the praise and thanksgiving? God will not share His glory with another. If we earnestly want God to answer our prayer, we must look to Him alone.

In his crying out to God, the psalmist makes two requests. First, *"hear me"* or *"answer me."* There seems to be an urgency here in that waiting will not suffice as an answer. There must be some resolution soon. His appeal is to the covenant-keeping God of Israel, the One who always keeps His promises. His promise to observe God's statutes is not a bribe but an affirmation that he will do as he has always done. Once the difficulty is resolved, he will not forget the Lord. God does answer prayer, and we must approach Him in humility, with repentance, and with right motives (II Chronicles 7:14; James 4:3) if we are truly earnest.

His second request when he cries out to the Lord is, *"save me."* Apparently, his life was in danger, but we are not given the specifics. Again, he promises to *"keep Your testimonies."* He is willing to do his part, which is the basis for expecting God's answer and deliverance. Why should God respond if a person is not willing to obey God's Word?

While praying earnestly in the night hours, we discern the second condition necessary to have confidence in the response of God. It is stated in two parts. The first is that he waits or hopes in God's words. He was praying in accordance with the revealed Word of God, which gave him the assured expectation that God would honour His Word. We usually do not pray earnestly unless we sincerely hope in God's Word. The second is that he meditates on God's promises throughout the night. How would he be able to pray in accordance with God's words if he had not been a student of God's promises? Why the emphasis on this activity at night? It shows his earnestness, and it was when he had free time to pray and meditate on the Word. The daylight hours were when he had to fulfil his responsibilities. I do not know of any employer who would give a day off for one of his employees to pray and meditate. The earnestness of our prayer is demonstrated in that we take the time available to us to cry out to God and not shirk our responsibilities. That may even mean we sacrifice a little sleep.

God is not concerned with how well we express ourselves in prayer, nor how long our prayers are, nor how many times we pray. He pays attention to the earnest petitioner as he prays sincerely.

Pray dependently (verses 149–150)
If we are praying with an undivided heart, we will be praying with full dependence on God. We depend on God's lovingkindness because we have no basis in demanding anything from Him. So many people have a concept of God as a cruel tyrant that punishes us whenever we take a wrong step. When we read the words of Jesus in the gospels, we are reassured that God is our heavenly Father who tenderly cares for His children. Even His discipline is meted out in love (Hebrews 12:5–11). Through faith in Jesus, we may approach our Father in heaven by appealing to His lovingkindness. He sees us as in His Beloved Son!

We depend on God's judgments because we know His judgments are always right and in accordance with His Word. It is almost as if the psalmist is saying, "Don't bend the rules on my behalf." So, he appeals to God's judgment for his life. Whether he is in danger of losing his life, or the vigour of life had drained from him because of his trial, he asks God to give him life (exuberance of life).

When faced with danger, we know we can depend on God. *"Those who follow after wickedness"* are those who devise schemes against God and the righteous. They are getting close to harming him in some way, but in doing so, they are far from the Law of God. His adversity is described in the briefest of words, but the seriousness is undiminished. The problem he faced was an enemy bent on doing evil who was far from God.

Pray confidently (verses 151–152)

The contrast is striking. The wicked were far from God's law, but the Lord is near, and all His commandments truly indicate the nearness of the Lord. God's commandments are truth, which means they are firm or certain. The personal, covenant-keeping Lord is near because He promises it in His Word. The commandments themselves are evidence of His nearness. Psalm 145:18 declares, *"The Lord is near to all who call upon Him, to all who call upon Him in truth,"* and Romans 8:16 says, *"the Spirit Himself testifies with our spirit that we are children of God."* The Spirit of God testifies within our hearts. He cannot be any nearer than that! God is not aloof.

Moreover, God's testimonies are eternally established. The psalmist says he has been aware of this truth for a long time. It indicates his confidence in a God who is near and whose testimonies have been established in eternity past. If established in eternity by an eternal God, they cannot be altered no matter how dire the psalmist's situation might be. God is near, and His Word, which is eternal, testifies to that!

1. When in distress, we are to pray earnestly, desiring God's help. Our earnestness will be evident from our commitment to God's Word and to our effort in internalizing the Word.

2. When in distress, we depend on God's lovingkindness and know His judgments are always right. We can leave our problems for God to deal with.

3. When in distress, we are convinced that God's commandments are certain so that when He says that He is with us, we know it is true. We are convinced that God's Word is eternally established and is therefore unchanging.

Psalm 119:153–160 — Resh

What To Pray When in Distress

ר

Resh.

153	Look upon my affliction and rescue me, For I do not forget Your law.
154	Plead my cause and redeem me; Revive me according to Your word.
155	Salvation is far from the wicked, For they do not seek Your statutes.
156	Great are Your mercies, O LORD; Revive me according to Your [judgments].
157	Many are my persecutors and my adversaries, *Yet* I do not turn aside from Your testimonies.
158	I behold the treacherous and loathe *them,* Because they do not keep Your word.
159	Consider how I love Your precepts; Revive me, O LORD, according to Your lovingkindness.
160	The sum of Your word is truth, And every one of Your righteous [judgments] is everlasting.[21]

---

[21] *New American Standard Bible: 1995 update.* 1995 (Psalm 119:153–160). LaHabra, CA: The Lockman Foundation.

In every life there are times of deep distress. It is God's desire that we lead victorious lives and not defeated lives. The previous stanza taught us how to pray when we are in distress, and this stanza answers the question of what we should pray when we are in distress. Our burdens drive us to our knees in prayer, and that is a privilege every Christian has. However, James 4:3 cautions us not to petition God with wrong motives to fulfil selfish desires. That seems obvious and simple, but if we were to examine thoroughly the reason for our requests in prayer, we might find that self-interests are more prevalent than we would care to admit.

A recurring phrase in these eight verses catches our attention, *"Revive me."* In verse 154 the psalmist says, *"Revive me according to Your word"*; in verse 156 we find, *"Revive me according to Your judgments"*; and then in verse 159, *"Revive me, O Lord, according to Your lovingkindness."* As I have noted before in this psalm the psalmist may be asking that his life be spared, but it could also be an appeal for the exuberance of life since his troubles have robbed him of his strength and zest for living. As we study this portion, we find a good illustration of salvation and the experience of the abundant life now as a result of our eternal life through salvation (John 10:10). God breathed the breath of life into the first man and imparted to him His life-giving Spirit. Sin destroyed that life, and through faith in Christ we are given that life again, only this time it vies for dominance in our lives with our sin nature. Everything in this world has the potential to appeal to our lower nature to rob us of the fulness of life the indwelling Spirit of God wants us to enjoy. Whenever we are in distress, that is the time to cry out for life as only God can give. This is not selfish as it is only when we are experiencing the life of God that God is glorified through us. It is possible to have the exuberance of life even in times of trials. To be bogged down in our sins and problems, with dejected looks on our faces, is not a good testimony of God's saving grace.

Give me life according to your promise (verses 153–155)

We who have trusted in Christ for our eternal salvation claim the many promises of God, such as John 3:36, *"He who believes in the Son has eternal life; but he who does not obey the Son will not see life, but the wrath of God abides on him."* This eternal life is experienced now in this life and more fully in the life to come. This verse, along with many others, is promised us in the Word.

The basis for the requests that follow is the psalmist has not forgotten the law of God, and he has not failed to act upon it. When God's Word is not foremost in our thinking, it is unlikely that we will be living according to it. So, the psalmist asks the Lord to look upon his affliction or misery. The appeal is to God's sympathy in the psalmist's misery suffered at the hands of his enemies and because he has not forgotten to act upon God's law. He has confidence in God's compassion, and He understands the struggle is a spiritual one. Miseries, in whatever form, come into a person's life to defeat him spiritually, which is accomplished when he takes his eyes off the Lord and the Word. But he had not forgotten God's law.

A second request is that the Lord would rescue or deliver him. He cries out for deliverance from those who are persecuting him, and he describes them as his adversaries in verse 157. It seems these adversaries were bringing false charges against him, so he asks the Lord to plead his cause. If the accusations stick, he would either lose his life or be incarcerated. We are reminded that we have an advocate with the father in the person of Jesus Christ (I John 2:1; Hebrews 9:24). Our adversary, the devil, may accuse us of many crimes, but Jesus, our advocate, pleads our justification on the basis of His death on the cross as a penalty for our sins.

Lastly, he asks the Lord to redeem him. The word "redeem" presents two beautiful pictures. First, the root word refers to a close relative who buys back some property or belongings to restore them to the original owner. The other picture is that of a purchase price that must be paid. The Lord is described as the redeemer of Israel. This would indicate His close relationship to the nation of Israel as her husband or father because of the covenant He made with her out of love. He redeemed Israel from Egypt and He redeems her from all her enemies. The purchase price in these situations was judgment on Israel's enemies (Isaiah 43:1–3). Here, the psalmist acknowledges his kinship with God and seeks deliverance from his adversaries through God's judgment on them.

For our eternal salvation, God saw our miserable sinful condition and rescued us. Now, Jesus, our advocate, pleads our case before God because He received the judgment for our sins and redeemed us as our close relative. We have eternal life and abundant life now because God heard our prayer of repentance and confession of Jesus as Lord and Savior of our lives.

In contrast to the godly psalmist, we read that the wicked are far from salvation because they do not seek God's statutes. Those described as wicked ignore the permanent feature of God's Word. They are the ones in distress and there is no deliverance for them. What a contrast between the psalmist, who does not forget God's law, and the wicked, who do not seek God's statutes! The lesson is plain. We cannot have confidence in God's help in times of distress if we are going to ignore His Word.

Give me life according to Your judgments (verses 156–158)
In considering the next two verses, we are struck by a significant comparison. The Lord's mercies are great, or many, while the psalmist's persecutors and adversaries are many. The psalmist appeals to the Lord to judge in his favour by giving him life. That would be to rescue him from his enemies or to revive his spirit. Because he claimed not to have forgotten God's law in contrast to the wicked, he could appeal to God's bountiful mercies.

Even though a large number of persecutors and adversaries were after him, he had not turned aside from following God's testimonies, or warning signs. So many times in distressing situations we try to take matters into our own hands while ignoring God's warning signs and reminders. Once we turn from God's testimonies (the Bible), we lose confidence in God's many mercies.

A further reaction to the psalmist's enemies is that he loathes them. He describes them as treacherous, but that is not the reason he loathes them. To loathe something is to have a profound disgust for it or be repulsed by it. The reason the psalmist feels this way towards them is not because of their animosity towards him. It is because they do not keep God's Word. They do not pay careful attention to it with the intent of abiding by it. Those who truly love the Lord and His Word will be repulsed by those who ignore God's Word. It is not the person, per se, but the activity that should disgust us.

In contrast to the treacherous, consider the following...

Give me life according to your lovingkindness (verses 159–160)
The word "consider" is the same word in verse 153 where it says, "look upon." We could render it this way, "look at how I love Your precepts." What would God see if we were to ask this of Him? Many claim to love God's Word, but what evidence is there to back the claim? When we ask God to take note of our love for His Word, He not only sees the activities that may indicate our love, but He also sees the motives and attitudes of the heart.

The psalmist makes this request so that the Lord would see the difference between him and
the treacherous. With a clear conscience, he appeals to God's scrutiny, knowing that God will judge rightly. Since he is confident in what God may find, he prays that the Lord would give him life according to God's lovingkindness.

The psalmist makes two statements that indicate his convictions regarding the Word of God that prompts his love for it. First, the sum total of God's Word is truth. When we are confident of the veracity of God's entire Word, we love it because we can trust it. Second, the psalmist describes individual statements of God's judgments as righteous and eternal. God's judgments are not for just one generation; they are appropriately correct for all of history. What was right for my grandparents and parents is right for me, my children, and my grandchildren. That should germinate a love for God's Word that drives me to read, study, meditate, and apply it over the course of my life.

Is there a slight amount of doubt as God scrutinizes the psalmist's heart that he appeals to the lovingkindness of the covenant-keeping God of Israel?

1. Give me life according to Your word (verse 154) is a dependence on the promises of God.
2. Give me life according to Your judgments (verse 156) is a request based on God's right administration of justice.
3. Give me life according to Your lovingkindness (verse 159) is a plea for God's tender love, knowing that, though he loves the Word of God, he is, nonetheless, undeserving because no one is without fault.

What do we pray when we are mired down in the afflictions of life? We pray for the abundant life that God gives us through faith in His Son. He gives it to us out of His promises, judgments, and lovingkindness. As the God who has made a new covenant with us through the blood of Jesus so that we are His children, He will grant this request!

Psalm 119:161–168 — Shin

The Word of God in the Believer's Life

שׁ

Shin.

161 Princes persecute me without cause,
But my heart stands in awe of Your words.

162 I rejoice at Your word,
As one who finds great spoil.

163 I hate and despise falsehood,
But I love Your law

.

164 Seven times a day I praise You,
Because of Your righteous [judgments].

165 Those who love Your law have great peace,
And nothing causes them to stumble.

166 I hope for Your salvation, O Lord,
And do Your commandments.

167 My soul keeps Your testimonies,
And I love them exceedingly.

168 I keep Your precepts and Your testimonies,
For all my ways are before You.[22]

For God's people, Israel, the Word of God was to hold a position of high priority in their everyday lives. The *shema,* taken from

---

[22] *New American Standard Bible: 1995 update.* 1995 (Psalm 119:161–168). LaHabra, CA: The Lockman Foundation.

Deuteronomy 6:4–9, states that the Lord (Yahweh) is God and that He is one. Therefore, God's people are to love Him with all their heart, soul, and strength. To enable them to keep this command, they were directed to keep God's Word continually in their hearts. They were to teach God's commands diligently to their children and *"bind them as a sign on your hand and they shall be as frontals on your forehead. You shall write them on the doorposts of your house and on your gates."* These instructions were probably to be taken metaphorically, meaning that God's Word was to be acted upon (hands), kept constantly in mind, and not left at home when one goes out of the house. The psalmist also does not live as a godly person only outside the home. The Jews of today take these words literally by wearing *phylacteries* and placing the *mezuzah* on the door posts. The lesson from this passage is that there is one God and only one God. He is to be loved with all of one's being. Total devotion to God cannot be maintained without the centrality of God's Word in a person's life.

What was true for the people of Israel is true for Christians today. The Bible must be central to our lives if we are to keep growing in our love and devotion to God. It all begins with our attitude towards the Bible.

The proper attitude towards the Bible (verses 161–163)
We begin with an attitude of awe of God's words. Awe is described as, "an overwhelming feeling of wonder or admiration" (American English Dictionary). However, the Hebrew word has the connotation of trembling or shaking with fear. It is not the pious fear of reverence or worship of God; that is another word. But it is a reverential trembling as described in Jeremiah 36:16, *"When they had heard all the words, they turned in fear one to another."* Other scripture verses couple this word with other synonyms for emphasis as in Jeremiah 33:9, Isaiah 19:16 and 33:14.

One would think the princes who were persecuting the psalmist without cause would produce fearful trembling in him, but it is God's Word that produces that kind of fear. Their threats did not deter him from respecting God's Word. When danger or calamity lurks around us, which may alarm us, we are to let the Word of God shake us more than that which alarms us.

Then we are told the psalmist rejoices at God's promise. His rejoicing is like one who has found great spoil after a hard-fought battle. In II Chronicles 20:20–26 we read the story of the Ammonites, Moabites, and Edomites joining together to wage war against King Jehoshaphat and Judah. Judah was very afraid, but Jehoshaphat led them in prayer to ask for God's help. The Lord caused the three invading armies to turn on each other, which resulted in a complete slaughter of Judah's enemies. All King Jehoshaphat and his army had to do was collect the spoils of war that were just lying there. We read that it took three days to gather up all the spoils, and on the fourth day they worshiped and blessed the Lord. They were praising God for the victory without having to fight and for all the spoils of war they had gained.

If King David was the author of this psalm, then one promise he rejoiced over is found in II Samuel 7 where God makes a covenant with David, promising him that his son would succeed him. That son would build the temple for the Lord. God also promised him that he would have an enduring dynasty. God has promised us who believe on His Son eternal life and life abundant. That is a promise, along with many others, in which to rejoice.

Finally, the psalmist says he loves God's law, which he contrasts to hating and despising falsehood. Since the law of God is truth, it is trustworthy. Lies are not to be trusted and can get us into trouble. God's Word is a reliable guide and will not lead us down the wrong path. It used to be that when traveling out in the countryside in India, there were very few signs to give direction. If you came to a fork in the road, you would ask someone for directions. The person giving you the directions, thinking he was doing you a favor, would try to anticipate the answer you wanted to hear so as not to disappoint you. If one road looked better than the other, he would direct you on that road, even if it took you miles out of your way. The wise traveler would go a short distance and ask again and then ask a third time farther down the road. It is better to hear the truth than what is pleasing. The Bible does not misdirect us just to make us feel happy. There is plenty in it to encourage us and give us joy, but there are also hard truths we cannot ignore, and those hard truths are for our good. If we love God's Word, we will follow it closely.

I can go into just about any room in my house and find a Bible. We have many versions, translations, paraphrases, and amplifications of the Bible. We, who are English speakers, are so blessed to have an abundance of Bibles in our own language. Just having a lot of Bibles is not helpful to us if we do not have an awe for God's Word, if we do not find real joy in reading it, or if we are not devoted out of love for it so that we read, study, and obey it.

The profound results from these attitudes (verses 164–166)
Once we have the right attitude towards the Word of God, we will be full of praise for God. Seven times a day might seem a bit much, but the point is probably not the number of times in a day we praise God but that we are constantly praising Him. As we meditate on God's righteous judgments, our hearts well up in continuous praise. God's judgments are right, and if we have a right attitude towards the Bible, we will naturally praise God.

We are told that when we love God's law, we will experience great peace. The biblical concept of peace is that our lives are in good order. There is a completion or perfection to our lives. Our love for God's Word results in our obedience to it, and when we follow God's Word, we find the truth sets us free from conflicts or confusion. *"If only you had paid attention to My commandments!*

Then your [peace] would have been like a river," says Isaiah in 48:18. The Word of God kept will keep us from stumbling into sin and sinful attitudes, and that is a recipe for peace.

When we do, or carry out, God's commandments, we are able to hope or wait for God's salvation or deliverance. We are not able to discern what the occasion is that requires salvation from God for the psalmist, but we can apply it to our salvation from sin. I may claim to be a believer in Jesus Christ and in His death on the cross to save me from sin, but if there is no change in my life regarding my obedience to the Word, any hope I may have will be a false hope, at best. Conversely, obedience is an outward sign of hope in our hearts or that we are expectantly awaiting the day of our salvation when Christ returns for us. I John 2:28–3:3 reinforces these truths.

The practical outworking of these attitudes (verses 167–168)
Our ardent love for God's testimonies (reminders, warning signs) motivates us to keep (diligently observe) them. When we think of how God's warning signs on life's pathway guides us safely through the obstacles our adversary lays out for us, we respond by loving God's Word exceedingly. This would be a love devoted to following the Bible through obedience.

A second motivation for keeping God's precepts (orders) and paying attention to His testimonies (warning signs) is we can never escape the scrutiny of God. Wherever we go, His presence is with us, and He knows every path we take. The Bible emphasizes the omniscience and omnipresence of God so that we will adhere to His revealed Word.

As a child, I was very aware that if my parents were to see my bad behaviour, I would be punished or reprimanded. This affected my view of God, that He was observing my behaviour to punish me when I got out of line. However, at this end of my life, I am more aware that His interest in me is not to punish but to bless me. My motivation for compliance to His Word is not out of fear of reprisal but out of rejoicing in His approval and gentle guidance when I do stray from the path that He would have me take. He gave us His Word to show us the way of blessing and peace, not to harm us. Sometimes it does take a firmer hand to set us on the right course again, but it is for our good.

Our attitude towards the Bible should be that of trembling awe intermingled with joy and love. When we have that kind of attitude, we experience a joyful heart of praise, a deep sense of wellbeing, and an assured hope in our eternal salvation. Therefore, I pay careful attention to the Word of God out of love for it and out of an awareness that God is present, watching over me for my good.

Psalm 119:169–176 — Tau

A Summary of Psalm 119

ת

Tav.

169   Let my cry come before You, O Lord;
       Give me understanding according to Your word.
170   Let my supplication come before You;
       Deliver me according to Your word.

171   Let my lips utter praise,
       For You teach me Your statutes.
172   Let my tongue sing of Your word,
       For all Your commandments are righteousness.

173   Let Your hand be ready to help me,
       For I have chosen Your precepts.
174   I long for Your salvation, O Lord,
       And Your law is my delight.

175   Let my soul live that it may praise You,
       And let Your [judgments] help me.
176   I have gone astray like a lost sheep; seek Your servant,
       For I do not forget Your commandments.[23]

---

[23] *New American Standard Bible: 1995 update.* 1995 (Psalm 119:169–176). LaHabra, CA: The Lockman Foundation.

This last stanza of Psalm 119 is a summation of all the psalmist has said throughout the psalm. It is my humble opinion that King David was the author of this psalm, but one cannot be dogmatic about it. David was known as a "man after God's own heart." A total devotion to the Word of God, as evidenced in Psalm 119, is key to being a man after God's own heart. God reveals His heart to sinful man through His Word. If we are going to know God, His ways, and His salvation, we must love the Word that He has graciously given us (verse 97). Drawing near to the heart of God can only be accomplished through communion with God by listening to God through the pages of His Word and by responding to Him with prayers of praise and supplication flowing from His speaking to us from His Word. So, the key to the heart of God comes through communion with God.

Two essential prayers for communion with God (verses 169–170)
While reading the Bible, we need to understand what we are reading. We discern an urgency in the psalmist's desire for understanding as he cries out to the Lord to pay attention to this request. As we have seen throughout this psalm, God is the one who gives us understanding, but we must do our part in reading, studying, meditating, and committing to obeying it if we expect God to answer this prayer. We need to understand the Bible so we can obey it fully and evaluate every event and circumstance from God's perspective. The apostle Paul urges us in Colossians 3:16, *"Let the word of Christ richly dwell in you"* and again in Romans 12:2 he says, *"and do not be conformed to this world, but be transformed by the renewing of your mind, so that you may prove what the will of God is, that which is good and acceptable and perfect."* The only way we can renew our minds is through the absorption of God's Word and allowing His Spirit to guide us in appropriating truth.

A second prayer reflects a common theme of this psalm, that is, a prayer for deliverance. The psalmist does not tell us from what he needs deliverance. Was it from enemies, illness, or some other danger? Throughout this psalm, we are made aware of a threat from the psalmist's enemies. It is hard to discern whether he is praying for deliverance through the trial or from the trial, but the word seems to be a request for rescue from an impossible situation. The focus of this verse, though, is his attitude in making this request. He does not demand it as the word "supplication" includes the concept of appealing to someone for a favor or for mercy. He reverently pleads that God would pay attention to his request. Furthermore, he asks for God's deliverance in accordance with God's promise. He appeals to what God has promised within His Word.

A man after God's own heart will pray earnestly for greater understanding of God's Word and for God's gracious assistance within the dictates of His Word. His prayers are reverential requests and not a demand as his trust is only in God.

One prerequisite disposition for communion with God (verses 171–172)

That one prerequisite is joy. The apostle Paul instructs us in Philippians 4:4, *"Rejoice in the Lord always, again I will say, rejoice!"* We have seen many verses in this psalm that describe the psalmist's fears, despair, and threats to his life, but through it all there is an abiding joy that comes from communion with God.

It is his desire that his lips would utter praise because, in answer to the prayer in verse 169, God has taught him the permanently inscribed-on-a-rock Word of God. The word "utter" means to pour out or to bubble forth. The praise cannot be restrained as he learns God's words that cannot be revoked or changed. Whenever we learn God's Word our hearts should well up in praise so that it cannot be kept back by closed lips. God's Word may cause sorrow, confusion, and maybe anger if we do not submit to its teachings. Surrendering to the revealed Word of God is the prescription for true joy. If learning God's Word does not result in praise, we must assume that the learning was inadequate or faulty but never because of a lack on God's part. It is evident that praise is in proportion to instruction.

Next, the psalmist sings for joy because God's commandments are righteous. The word "sing" means to answer, speak, or testify in response to something. When God gives understanding through His teaching of the Word, hearts respond by testifying to others of God's righteous commandments. Singing is an appropriate way of reaffirming the truths of the Bible. God's promises are something to testify, or sing, about, and praise pours out when God instructs us. One can imagine the barrier a downcast disposition would have in communing with God.

Two necessary commitments for communion with God (verses 173–174)
When one chooses God's precepts (orders) for his life, he does so after careful examination. God never expects us to have a blind faith as we are often accused of having. God has given us His Word so it can be examined and put to the test, and His Word will withstand any test we give it. However, choosing to make God's precepts our guide and rule for life does not mean we will always be obedient. The prayer for God's help recognizes the weakness of our will. God's power, symbolized by His hand, in our lives is a necessity if we are going to keep our commitment.

God's hand is *ready* to help, which pictures a child learning to walk with a parent's hand hovering over him to catch him when (not if) he falls. "Lord, keep Your hand ready to steady me while I endeavor to walk according to Your precepts." We cannot expect or ask God to help if we do not determine to follow His orders.

Not only should we choose God's precepts, but we should also long for His salvation. The covenant-keeping God has promised to preserve us for His glory, whether for eternal salvation or for deliverance from our temporal afflictions. In either case, we long for it, which is proved by our delight in His law. A longing for the Lord's salvation would indicate we are not trusting in our own devices, nor in anything or anyone else. If our focus is on His salvation, we will not be wandering aimlessly.

The Lord Jesus asked His disciples in John 6:67, *"You do not want to go away also, do You?"* to which Peter replied in verse 68, *"Lord, to whom shall we go? You have the words of eternal life."*

Communion with God demands that we choose Him and long for His salvation. In our frailty we ask Him to be ready to help us. Our hope is in His salvation, so we find our delight in His law. We are not looking elsewhere as He has the words of eternal life.

One primary request for communion with God (verses 175–176)
In these last two verses the primary request of the psalmist is that God would let his soul live. He is asking either for eternal salvation or for the fulness of life that only God can give in the ups and downs of life. Judging from the overall context of this psalm, I would lean toward the latter understanding; however, the former is very much a possibility and is reasonable. He prays this so that he may praise the Lord. When his soul is burdened with the afflictions of life, it is difficult to praise Him. Also, a dead person cannot praise the Lord among men, though he certainly will in the presence of God in glory.

So that his soul may live, the psalmist appeals to the Lord for help through God's judgments. This would indicate a need for understanding God's judgments so they can help us. God's Word is available to us for our understanding, and with the understanding we apply God's truth to our lives. The application of God's truth increases our joy in life.

Now, for the only time in this psalm, we have any acknowledgment of wrongdoing. In a picture that reminds us of Isaiah 53:6 and the parable of the lost sheep in Luke 15:4–7, the psalmist describes a condition that is common to man. We have all wandered from time to time from the paths of the Good Shepherd. In praying that the Lord would seek him out, it would seem it was not a deliberate departure but a wandering away until he recognizes he has lost his way. In his lost condition, he claims that he had not forgotten God's commandments. By not forgetting them, he continued to follow them, but his conduct would not have been pleasing to the Lord. Therefore, he would have been out of fellowship with the Lord, and his experience of the abundant life was lacking. When the experience of eternal life is lacking in the believer, there is a lack of assurance of salvation and a fear of reprisal. It is appropriate to cry out, *"let my soul live that I may praise You."*

The Christian faces a constant battle with the temptations of the flesh as Galatians 5:16–17 tells us. Someone, like the psalmist, who loves the Lord and His Word, will not be willing to lose the sweet communion with God for long. Being a Christian does not mean we never fail, but it does mean we will yield to the Lord's conviction by repenting and receiving His forgiveness. Continuance is the evidence of genuine faith in Christ. God seeks those who remember (act upon) His Word instead of condemning them. We can be assured that our communion with God is just as precious to Him as it is to us, if not more so.

To be people after God's own heart, we will be praying for more understanding of God's Word and for deliverance from that which would cause us to forfeit the life God has promised us in Christ Jesus. It also means we will be so absorbed by the Scriptures that our joy will bubble up spontaneously. We will have a resolute heart to choose the Bible for our lives and to look to God alone for salvation. In our humility we will seek God's mercy for our constant failures.

It is a trustworthy statement:
For if we died with Him, we will also live with Him;
If we endure, we will also reign with Him;
If we deny Him, He also will deny us;
If we are faithless, He remains faithful,
For He cannot deny Himself.

II Timothy 2:11–13

Bibliography

Barnes, Albert. (1769) *Psalm 119, Notes on the Old Testament,* Grand Rapids: Baker Book House.

_____. (1940) *C. H. Spurgeon's Treasury of David Vol. 2,* Condensed by David Otis Fuller.

Delitzsch, F. (1986) *Keil & Delitzsch Commentary on the Old Testament, Vol. 5,* Peabody: Hendrickson Publishers.

Holladay, William. (1971) *A Concise Hebrew and Aramaic Lexicon of the Old Testament.* Grand Rapids: Wm. B. Eerdmans.

Kidner, Derek. (1975) *Tyndale Old Testament Commentaries — Psalms Vol. 2.* General Editor D. J. Wiseman. Downers Grove: Inter-Varsity Press.

_____. (1971) *The Pulpit Commentary.* H. D. M. Spence, Josephs, and Excell editors. Grand Rapids: Eerdmans.

_____. (1980) *Theological Wordbook of the Old Testament.* R. Laird Harris, Gleason L. Archer, Jr., Bruce K. Waltke, Editors. Chicago: Moody Press.

Van Gemeren, William A. (1991) *Psalms — The Expositor's Bible Commentary;* Frank E. Gabelein, General Editor, Grand Rapids: Zondervan.

_____. (1976) *The Zondervan Pictorial Encyclopedia of the Bible;* Merrill C. Tenney, Editor. Grand Rapids: Zondervan Publishing House.

Appendix — Study Outlines

Psalm 119:1-8 Aleph
God's Personal Attention

God demonstrates His love for us through His personal attention.

I. God delights in our righteousness (1-3)
    (by blessing us)
    A.   Undefiled in the way

    B.   Keep His testimonies

II. God demands our obedience (4)
    (by ordering us)
    A. Authority

    B. Responsibility

III. God desires our perseverance (5-8)
    (by being faithful to us)
    A. The necessity of a personal desire

    B. The necessity of a personal determination

Psalm 119:9-16 Beth
The Well-balanced Christian Life

The godly man demonstrates his love for God.

I. He demonstrates a concern for righteousness (9-11)
>   A. Purity (9)

>   B. Prayer (10)

>   C. Purpose (11)

II. He demonstrates a continual rejoicing (12-14)
>   A. Praise (12)

>   B. Proclamation (13)

>   C. Perspective (14)

III. He demonstrates a consecrated resolve (15,16)
>   A. Determination (15)

>   B. Delight (16)

Psalm 119:17-24 Gimel
The Prayers of a Godly Person

The pursuit of God puts into perspective our earthly relationships.

I. Our prayers concerning our relationship to God (17-20)
    A. The prayer for God's goodness (17)

    B. The prayer for spiritual vision (18-20)

II. Our prayer concerning our relationship to others (21-24)
    A. A preliminary observation (21)

    B. A prayer for deliverance (22)

    C. Reasons for the prayer (23,24)

Psalm 119:25-32 Daleth
God's way and the life of the believer.

God's way meets our deepest needs through the Word.

I. The Way of Life (25,26)
        Two hindrances to life
    A.   Dependency on the transitory (25)

    B.   Deceitfulness of the human heart (26)

II. The Way of Victory (27-29)
    A.   Victory over pride (27)

    B.   Victory over heartache (28)

    C.   Victory over deceit (29)

III. The Way of Truth (30-32)
    A.   Choose it (30)

    B.   Stick to it (31)

    C.   Be devoted to it (32)

Psalm 119:33-40 He
Causal Clauses of Commitment:

The Godly man recognizes the aids and hindrances for spiritual life.

I. Causes for Obedience (33-35)
    A.   Teach me

    B.   Give me understanding

    C.   Make me walk

II. Causes for Disobedience (36-39)
    A.   Money

    B.   Idols

    C.   Doubt

    D.   Disgrace

III. Causes for eternal life (40)
    A.   Man's part

    B.   God's part

Psalm 119:41-48 Vav
Prayers and Promises

The prayers and promises of a man in tune with God.

I. A prayer for God's Mercies (41,42)
    A.   Mercies = loving-kindness/ salvation

    B.   Result of God's mercies

II. A prayer for the availability of God's Word (43-46)
    A.   It is my hope

    B.   It is my eternal guide

    C.   It is my strength

III. Three promises concerning God's word (47,48)
    A.   I will delight myself

    B.   I will lift up my hands

    C.   I will meditate

Psalm 119:49-56 Zayin
The Transforming Word of God

The internalized Word of God transforms us.

I. When God acts upon His Word we experience hope (49-52)
Verse 49 is a plea that God would not forget His promises as he has placed all his hope (confidence) in them. This hope is displayed in the comfort he experiences particularly in two situations.

    A.   The Word produces comfort in affliction

    B.   The Word produces comfort in ridicule

II. When we act upon His Word we exhibit Christ-likeness (53-56)
Verse 56 – verses 53-55 are a result of keeping God's precepts

    A.   The Word kept produces horror of sin

    B.   The Word kept produces joy

    C.   The Word kept produces love

Psalm 119:57-64 Cheth
A Longing for God's Loving-kindness

We demonstrate a longing for God's loving-kindness in our lives.

I. We pray for God's grace (favour) (57,58)
The last phrase of verse 2 says "Be merciful unto me according to thy Word." Cf. vs. 17, 41

    A.   The Lord is our portion

    B.   The Word is our rule

    C.   The Lord is our God

II. We repent of our ways (59, 60)

    A.   We take a good look at our ways

    B.   We hurry back to God

III. We exhibit new loyalties (61-63)

    A.   Loyalty to the Word in the midst of the ungodly

    B.   Loyalty to the Lord in secret

    C.   Loyalty to other believers

IV. We perceive God's loving-kindness (64)

Psalm 119:65-72 Teth
God is Good

God uses affliction to teach us the value of His Word.

I. We evaluate the many facets of God's goodness. (65-68)
    A.   It is always according to His Word

    B.   It requires prayer and conviction to discern

    C.   It is sometimes experienced through affliction

    D.   It is an extension of God's character

II. We experience the depth of God's goodness (69-72)
    A.   Learning obedience is an expression of God's goodness

    B.   Learning the value of God's law is an expression of God's goodness.

Psalm 119:73-80 Yodh
The Strength of the Afflicted

We use adversity to demonstrate our spiritual strength.

I. We demonstrate a godly attitude (73-75)
    A.   God made us

    B.   Men rejoice in our hope

    C.   Personal convictions

II. We demonstrate a dependence on God (76-77)
    A.   For God's merciful kindness for comfort

    B.   For God's tender mercies for life

III. We demonstrate wisdom in seeking counsel (78-79)
    A.   Counsel of the arrogant

    B.   Counsel of the godly

IV. We demonstrate a spiritual resolve (80)
    A.   For a blameless heart

    B.   For a shameless life

Psalm 119:81-88 Kaph
Getting a Grip on Reality

The Word of God provides the bridge between our afflictions and the reality that is God.

I. Description of his condition (81-83)
    A.   Emotions

    B.   Intellect

    C.   Physical body

II. Description of his afflictions (84-87)
    A.   Unanswered questions

    B.   Undeserved persecutions

    C.   Near destruction

III. Description of his salvation (deliverance) (88)
    A.   The basis of salvation

    B.   The purpose of salvation

Psalm 119:89-96 Lamedh
The Eternality of the Word

Since the Word of God is rooted in God's eternality we can have complete confidence in it.

I. The Proposition – God's word is eternal (89)
  A.   Forever it stands firm

  B.   In heaven it stands firm

II. The Examples (90-91)
  A.   God is faithful towards people

  B.   God is faithful towards the earth

  C.   God is faithful towards all creation

III. The Applications (92-95)
  A.   For our salvation/deliverance

  B.   For our life experiences

IV. The Conclusion (96)
  A.   All perfection has a limit

  B. God's Word has no limits

Psalm 119:97-104 Mem
Loving God's Word

Our love for the Word of God will be demonstrated in tangible ways.

I. The Prevailing Attitude of Love for God's Word (97)

    A.   The Exclamation

    B.   The Evidence

II. The Result of Loving God's Word (98-100)

    A.   Wiser than my enemies

    B.   More understanding than all my teachers

    C.   Understand more than the ancients

III. The Demonstration of Love for God's Word (101-102)

    A.   Watch my steps

    B.   Not departed from God's judgments

IV. The Rewards of Loving God's Word (103-104)

    A.   It is pleasant

    B.   I get understanding

Psalm 119:105-112 Nun
A Creed to Follow

We experience guidance for our lives when we are devoted to God's Word.

I. A Promise to Keep (105-106)
    A.   The acknowledgement

    B.   The perseverance

II. Obstacles to Overcome (107-110)
    A.   Affliction

    B.   Danger

    C.   Deception

III. A Future to claim (111-112
    A.   A choice of an inheritance

    B.   An inclination of the heart

Psalm 119:113-120 Samech
The Battle is the Lord's

In our daily struggles we dare not take God for granted.

I. The Battle (113-115)

    A.   The opponents

    B.   The defense

    C.   The mindset

II. The Resource (116-117)

    A.   Prayer for support

    B.   Prayer for deliverance

III. The Victory (118-119)

    A.   The enemy defeated

    B.   The enemy judged

IV. The Reaction (120)

Psalm 119:121-128 Ayin
When God Acts

God acts according to our activities and His Word.

I. Activities that ensure God's protection (121-123)
    A.   The activities of the righteous

        1.   Judgment

        2.   Justice (Righteousness)

    B.   The response expected from God
        1.   Do not leave me

        2.   Be surety for me

        3.   Do not let the proud oppress me

    C.   The attitude of the righteous

II. Activity of God that ensures further obedience (124-125)
    A.   The prayer for the Lord's action
          Based on the Lord's loving-kindness
          - Teach me thy statutes

    B.   The prayer for the Lord's action
        Based on his attitude as a servant
        - Give me understanding for the knowledge of God's testimonies

III. Activity of God in judgment of the disobedient (126-128)
   A. God's judgment
      1. The time is right

      2. Against those who break God's law

   B. The reaction to God's judgment
      1. I love thy commandments

      2. I esteem <u>all</u> thy precepts

      3. I hate <u>every</u> false way

'Ye that love the Lord, hate evil.'
He that loves a tree hates the worm that consumes it.
He that loves a garment hates the moth that eats it.
He that loveth life abhoreth death;
And he that loves the Lord hates everything that offends Him.
Let men take heed to this, who are in love of their sins:
How can the love of God be in them?

                                        William Cowper

Psalm 119:129-136 Pe
The Transforming Power of God's Word

The study of God's Word transforms our attitudes.

I. Transforming my attitude towards the Word of God (129-131)
    A.   Response to the intrinsic value of God's Word

    B.   Response to the effective value of God's Word

II. Transforming my attitude towards prayer (132-135)
    A.   Prayer for God's favour

    B.   Prayer for victory over temptation

    C.   Prayer for freedom to obey God

    D.   Prayer for God's instruction

III. Transforming my attitude towards sinners (136)

Psalm 119:137-144 Tsadhe
Some Intrinsic Qualities of God's Word

The intrinsic qualities of God's Word stirs my heart with zeal.

I. The reliability of God's Word (137-139)
- A.   Why?
  - 1.

  - 2.

  - 3.

- B.   Result

II. The Purity of God's Word (140-141)
- A.   Why?

D. Result

III. The Eternality of God's Word (142-144)
- A.   Why?
  - 1.

  - 2.

  - 3.

- B.   Result

Psalm 119:145-152 Qoph
How To Pray When in Distress

Effective prayers will be consistent with the Word of God.

I. Pray Earnestly (145-148)
    A.   Cry with the whole heart
        1.   Hear me

        2.   Save me

    B.   Pray during the night hours
        1.   Cried before the dawn

        2.   Meditated in the Word during the night

II. Pray Dependently (149-150)
    A.   Dependent on God's
        1.   Loving kindness

        2.   Judgments

    B.   Dependent because of danger

III. Pray Confidently (151-152)
    A.   God's commandments are <u>truth</u>

    B.   God's testimonies are <u>eternally established</u>

Psalm 119:153-160 Resh
What To Pray When in Distress

In times of distress we cry out for life as only God can give.

I. Give me life according to your promise (153-155)
- A.   I do not forget your law
  - 1.   Consider my misery

  - 2.   Deliver (save) me

  - 3.   Defend my cause

  - 4.   Redeem me

- B.   They do not seek your statutes
  - Salvation is far from the wicked

II. Give me life according to your judgments (156-158)
- A.   The great comparison
  - 1.   Many are your tender mercies

  - 2.   Many are my persecutors and enemies

- B.   The great response
  - 1.   I do not turn from your testimonies

  - 2.   I loath the treacherous
    - Because they do not keep your word

III. Give me life according to your lovingkindness
  - Consider how I love your precepts
- A.   The sum total of your Word is true

- B.   The individual parts of your judgments are
  - 1.   Righteous

  - 2.   Eternal

Psalm 119:161-168 Shin
The Word of God in the Believer's Life

We give the Word of God a central place in our lives.

I. The Proper Attitude towards the Bible (161-163)
    A.   Awe

    B.   Joy

    C.   Love

II. The Profound Result from these attitudes (164-166)
    A.   Praise

    B.   Peace

    C.   Hope

III. The Practical Outworking of these attitudes (167-168)
    A.   Keep out of love

    B.   Keep out of "fear"

Psalm 119:169-176 Tau
A Summary of Psalm 119

The key to the heart of God comes through communion with God.

I. Two essential prayers for communion with God (169, 170)
    A.   The need for understanding

    B.   The need for deliverance

II. One pre-requisite disposition for communion with God (171, 172) – Joy
    A.   Praise for instruction from God

    B.   Sing for joy because God's commandments are righteous.

III. Two necessary commitments for communion with God (173,174)
    A.   Choose God's precepts

    B.   Long for God's salvation

IV. One primary request in order to have communion with God (175, 176) "Let my soul live"
    A.   Let your judgments help me

    B.   Seek your servant

Made in USA - North Chelmsford, MA
76724_9781681115535
02.21.2024 1328